ANCIENT AFRICA

2 books in 1

African Mythology and Ancient African Kingdoms

Jim Barrow

To thank you for your purchase, we're offering a free PDF exclusively for the readers of Ancient Africa – 2 books in 1: African Mythology and Ancient African Kingdoms

Dive into the Ancient Civilization and their Gods: Reveal the Secrets of the Egyptian Civilization Going Back 5000 Years B.C. & Learn the Myths That Created their Culture.

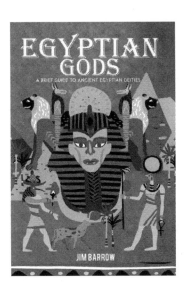

Scan the following QR Code to access your free gift!

TABLE OF CONTENTS

Chapter 3 The story of ancient Africa at the dawn.... 43

Chapter 4 Gods and goddesses from the African continent 63

Chapter 5 Legends with animals as protagonists 89

Chapter 6 Legends with heroes as protagonists 100

Chapter 7 Creation myths and legends from Africa 109

Book 1

AFRICAN MYTHOLOGY

Gods, Heroes, Legends and Myths of Ancient Africa

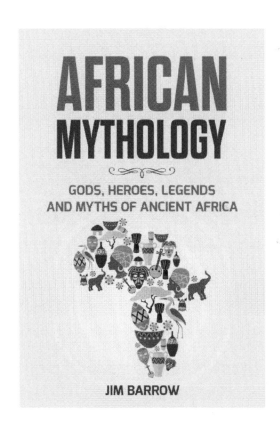

Scan the following QR Code to have the audiobook of "African Mythology" for free!

Chapter 1

General overview of african mythology

Mythology

Mythology is basically the study of myths. A myth is a story that people believe is true since it is usually connected to the history of the people. According to Encyclopedia Britannica (1133), a myth is "a story handed down in oral form from our forefathers which explains reality, concepts, and beliefs and further serves as explanations of nature and events such as creations, the origin of things, history of a race or a people."

Abu Nuwas (ca 756-ca 814)

Abu Nuwas, also Abu Nowas or Abu Nu'as, was a Persian poet in the 8th century who became a trickster-hero in the region of East Africa where Arabic culture is most dominant such as Madagascar, Mauritius, Tanzania, and Zanzibar. Abu Nuwas al-Hasan was his full name, and he was born in al-Ahwaz, Persia – now known as Ahvaz, Iran. The kalifs, Harun al-Rashid and his son, al-Amin both favored him, and he was quite successful at the Baghdad court up till the day he died. In the golden age of Arabic literature, Abu Nuwas is recognized as one of the great poets whose verse is said to be creative and combines humor and irony. It was his sense of humor and the continual quest for pleasure that made him appear in over one hundred myths as a trickster and jester. He was one of the characters in The Thousand and One Nights, which is also known as the Arabian Nights' Entertainment, a collection of myths from India, Arabia, and Persia.

A story of how his ingenuity entertained his supporters goes thus: On a certain day, Abu Nuwas visited the sultan while weeping and informed the sultan that his wife passed away. The sultan then promised that another wife would be found for him; the sultan's wife (sultana) brought him a maiden, and both Abu Nuwas and the maiden decided to get married. The couple received a lot of gifts from the sultan and 1,000 pieces of gold. Abu Nuwas and his wife were too carefree with their spending that they spent all the money they had received from the sultan. While in that situation, Abu Nuwas came up with a strategy to get money. He visited the sultan to tell him that his new wife had passed, but he didn't possess the funds to entomb her; this made the sultan give him 200 pieces of gold.

His wife, on the other hand, went on to inform the sultana that her husband was dead and that she lacked the funds to entomb him, and the sultana gave her 200 pieces of gold. That evening, when the sultan and sultana met, she informed the sultan that Abu Nuwas was dead; the sultan argued, saying that it was Abu Nuwas' wife that died. To resolve the situation, a servant was sent to the house of Abu Nuwas to see who was actually dead.

On getting to the house, the servant saw Abu Nuwas' wife lying 'dead' as Abu Nuwas had made her lie down and covered her with a sheet to make it look like her corpse. Doubting the report, the sultana sent a second servant who this time saw the corpse of Abu Nuwas, who had laid down and covered himself with a sheet, feigning to be dead.

Determined to investigate, both the sultana and sultan went Abu Nuwas and saw the supposed corpses of the couple; the sultan then made a decree that he would give 1,000 pieces of gold to anybody who would be able to reveal exactly what had happened. Hearing this, Abu Nuwas got up and told the sultan to give him the money; this made the sultan and sultana break into laughter, seeing that they had been clearly deceived. The sultan then gave Abu Nuwas the money.

Abu Yazid (Abuyazidu) (d. 947)

Abu Yazid, also, Abu Yazidu is a mythical hero of the Berber people of Algeria, Morocco, and Tunisia. He was the leader of one of the Berber folks, the tribe of Zanata. He spread the Kharajide faith across North Africa after taking it up and converting the people of his tribe to the religion. Because of this, conflict arose between him and the Fatimid kalifs, who at that time were the rulers of North Africa. Abu Yazid subdued a lot of significant towns when the Fatimid kalif, Imam al-Qaim was in power (933–945); this made the kalif to escape, seeking sanctuary in Mehdiya, a city in Morocco where Abu Yazid came and laid siege in the year 945.

Although Abu Yazid did not succeed in conquering the city after laying the siege, Imam al-Qaim was killed while the siege lasted. al-Mansur, the son of the Imam, took over from him, and although Abu Yazid's rebellion was great, al-Mansur was able to quench it. Abu Yazid then had to retreat to Susa. While Abu Yazid was in Susa, al-Mansur launched another attack at him, forcing him to seek refuge in Morocco, although he did not stop revolting against al-Mansur. It was later at Fort Kutama that Abu Yazid was discomfited and wounded while in battle. He died a few moments later. In spite of their differences, Abu Yazid was highly respected by al-Mansur so much that after Abu Yazid died, his family was catered for by al-Mansur.

Aiwel Longar

The mythical hero that is thought of as the ancestor of the Bor people, Dinka, Sudan, is named Aiwel Longar. Stories talk about Aiwel Longar. Some of the stories are regarded as enfant terrible stories – that is, stories that are about people who were borne in a strange way and possessed superhuman abilities.

One myth that talks about the life of Aiwel goes thus: A woman who only had a daughter was weeping because she had no male child, and her husband had passed away. A river god felt sorry for her and, with his waters, got her pregnant. The child she gave birth to was born with a full set of teeth, which signified that he had supernatural powers, and the woman named him Aiwel.

Although still a child, Aiwel was able to walk and speak, and when the mother found out about it, he warned her not to reveal it to anybody; when she did, she dropped dead. Then, Aiwel departed to live with the river god, who was his father until he grew up, after which he came back to the village where he was born with an ox having every last color on its skin. He came to be known by the name of his ox – Aiwel Longar after he had returned; he then took the herd of cattle that belonged to his mother's husband.

A time came when there were famine and drought in the land; the cattle belonging to the other villagers started to grow thin and eventually began to die. Aiwel's cattle, however, remained healthy and fat. Curious, a few young men decided to spy on him to uncover what was behind the health of his cattle and discovered that whenever Aiwel touched the ground, grass and water came up.

The young men described what they witnessed; all of them dropped dead. Aiwel then told the villagers that they had to leave the village in order to get away from the famine, offering to take them to a place that had many supplies to sustain them, but the villagers turned him down and went their own way.

When the people attempted to travel across a river, Aiwel started throwing spears at them, but one man was able to get close enough to hold Aiwel down until he could not move. Then, Aiwel permitted the people to get across, gave them his spears, and told them that he would depart and never return except when they needed his help.

Another version of this myth says that an old woman whose only child was a girl survived by catching fish in the river. A day came when she a certain creature in the river swashed water on her, and she became pregnant, but she did not give birth until after eight years – she gave the boy the name Aiwel; because the woman was well past the age of childbirth, the daughter refused to accept Aiwel as a brother.

Therefore, Aiwel began to live as a castaway who survived by keeping the cattle of the chief. The chief by the name of Fadol gave him a cow that became pregnant and gave birth to a yellow calf and eventually grew and became a spotted bull. This is why Aiwel came to be known as Aiwel-Longar. When a time of famine and drought came, every cattle in the land started getting thin and were dying except for the cattle of Fadol, which were being taken care of by Aiwel.

One day, Fadol followed Aiwel without his notice and saw that Aiwel hit the ground, and water and grass came out of it. Immediately Aiwel saw him, Fadol dropped dead, but Aiwel touched him and brought him back to life. The two of them went back to the village, and Fadol gifted Aiwel with several cattle and two beautiful women to become his wives. After Fadol passed, Aiwel became the chief, and his spear symbolized his power and divinity. Today, the priests of the clan of spear masters are said to have descended from him; the priests are the intermediaries between the gods and the people, and they are known to have killed the sacrificial oxen with spears.

Akoma Mba

Akoma Mba is of Fang origin, Cameroon, Equatorial Guinea, and Gabon. He was a Fang epos hero whose story showed that his behavior was not considered normal. As a child, he demonstrated his distinctness amongst other unique children who had supernatural powers. However, his behavior could no longer be predicted, and he eventually became a cause of pain to his family. Later in life, he became a warrior that was widely known who had a lot of conquests with various people, and in the end, he became king over the Ekang people.

Antar (ca. 525–615)

Antar, also Antara or Antarah, is a myth of the Bedouin people of Algeria, Libya, Morocco, and Western Sahara. Antar was a famous hero, poet, and a warrior who was born as a slave but then rose to become a headman. His full name was Antarah ibn Shaddad al-Absi, and because of his great acts, several legends were written and told about him in the Arabic epos known as Sirat Antar, meaning Romance of Antar.

He was wealthy, magnanimous, benevolent, and brave – a perfect representation of what a Bedouin chief should be. He wasn't born into leadership; instead, he achieved it through his strong sense of character and herculean spirit; he was a defender of people who were weak (suffering) and was very famous because of his bravery and valor. Legend has it that Anatar's mother was an Ethiopian slave, and Shaddad, the chief of the tribe of Abs was his father; but he was treated like a slave because he was not acknowledged as the chief's son. When he became 15 years old, he demonstrated his abilities as a warrior, and as a reward, the Shaddad granted him his freedom. Antar later became the chief of his tribe, and he was celebrated as a poet of his generation just as he is by modern-day critics. Despite not being a Muslim, one of the poems he wrote was awarded the highest honor that an Islamic writer could have, and it is exhibited at the entrée of the temple at Mecca.

As the epic, Sirat Antar narrates, Antar did not know that his father was the headman. He fell in love with his cousin Ibla (or Abla) and kept writing her love poems; annoyed by this, Malik, her father, and Antar's uncle consulted with Shaddad (the chief) and planned to have Antar killed. The reason they changed their plans was that they witnessed Antar put down a lion with bare hands.

When Antar found out that the chief was his father, he requested to be acknowledged as the chief's son, but the chief beat him up and threw him out. Antar then went on a quest, which is usually embarked on by epic heroes. Legend claims that he fought the king of Ethiopia and that Algeria and Morocco was part of his conquests. He also struggled and survived spirits and other spiritual forces as his quest took him outside North Africa unto Iraq, Iran, Syria, and Rome.

He had a lot of wealth during his return and didn't relent on his pursuit to marry Ibla despite how much her family resisted him. He went as far as killing a rival before her family finally gave up, and he took her to him home in a palanquin.

Bayajida

Bayajida is a fabled hero of the Hausa people of Niger and Nigeria. There are some stories of history that say he was the son of the king of Baghdad. Bayajida's Arabic name was Abuyazidu; hence, the claim that through Bayajida, the Hausas descended originally from the Arabs. Abuyazidu had a great army under his command, and after fighting a great battle against foes that launched an attack against Baghdad, he and his army roamed their way into Bornu in the northern part of Nigeria. On reaching Bornu, he and the sultan became allies, and together, they fought against any enemy that threatened Bornu territory. The people of Bornu gave him the name Bayajida, and he soon married Magira, the daughter of the sultan.

Bayajida grew popular, and he had a lot of wealth and power. This made the sultan jealous of him, and he tried to kill him. Magira found out about her father's plot and warned her husband, and both she and her husband escaped together. When they got to Garum Gabas, Magira discovered that she was pregnant, so Bayajida left her there and continued to travel until he got to a town known as Daura, which was under the rulership of a woman called Daurama.

An old woman let him take refuge in her house, and when he asked her for some water, she said that she didn't have any. The town only had one well from which to draw water, but a great snake lived inside the well, and the only way the villagers could draw water was if they all gathered together into a group of people that were strong enough to hold back the snake.

The woman's story didn't faze Bayajida as he took a bucket and went to the well and started to draw water. While drawing out the bucket, the snake clutched to the rope that it was tied to the bucket. With one of his hands, Bayajida grabbed the head of the snake and chopped it off. He dropped the body of the snake by the side of the well, but he took its head, put it in his bag, and headed back to the woman's house.

The following morning, the people saw the body of the snake lying dead around the well and took the news to their queen. The queen then made a decree that half her town will be given to the person who killed the snake. Many people claimed that they were the ones who had killed the snake, but none of them were able to provide proof (the snake's head). The woman who had been housing Bayajida went to the queen and told her about him and all that had happened, and then, the queen called for him.

When he got there, he showed her the head of the snake, and the queen proceeded to give him half of her town, but he declined. He insisted that she married him. The queen agreed, and they lived happily for a long time and had a son named Bawo. When they both died, Bawo ruled Daura in their stead; he had six sons, and they founded and ruled six of the seven Hausa states. The seventh Hausa state was founded by Bayajida's son from his first wife, Magira.

Ditaolane

Ditaolane, also Lituolone, is a diviner of the Sotho people residing in Lesotho. He is a mythical hero who had spiritual powers, and the story of his birth was strange. When Ditaolane was to be born, a fearful creature known as Kammapa was at the verge of devouring every human being. The only woman alive was the mother of Ditaolane, who was hiding at the time.

After Ditaolane was born, there were charms of divination about his neck. This was why his mother named him Ditaolane, meaning Diviner. Within the short period of time that his mother spent in gathering straw to make him a bed, Ditaolane had already grown to be an adult and was able to speak as though he was a sage. Noticing that the world was empty, he asked his mother why it was so, and she told him of Kammapa. So, taking a knife, Ditaolane went looking for the beast, and when he found Kammapa, he was swallowed whole though unharmed.

From the inside of the beast, Ditaolane used his knife to cut its intestines, and Kammapa died; then, Ditaolane cut open the beast's body from the inside so he could come out. Everyone who had been consumed before also came out with Ditaolane. Instead of thanking him, the people were afraid of him and even planned to have him killed, but because of his divination skills, he knew of their plot in advance, and the plan of the people failed.

He was being chased by his foes one day when he turned himself into a stone; one of the people chasing him became frustrated that they could not find him and picked up the stone and plunged it across a river. Ditaolane transformed back into himself and then continued his journey. A different version says that time came where he became weary of running to save himself, and he eventually surrendered to the people chasing him, and they killed him. After his death, his heart turned into a bird and flew out of his body.

Ebele

Ebele is a mythical hunter in the myths of the Igbo people of Nigeria. The Igbos think of Ebele as their ancestor even though there was no one that knew exactly where he came from. It is said that he just came out of nowhere and decided to reside in Ohanko (a town). During the intervening period, Ohanko happened to be at war with two other different towns towards the south, and so many people lost their lives in the process because while the war went on, the armies were fighting with spears and arrows that had been poisoned.

Ebele, on the other hand, had a firelock rifle, and with it, he went to fight for the Ohanko people, and most of their enemies died from his gunfire. Also, among the enemies were people who never came across a gun before. They were unaware of its capabilities and seeing things as though their brothers died because the weapon was powered by magic, they ran away in panic.

Ebele was heralded as the savior of the town of Ohanko, and the people made him a high occupant of their town. A couple of years after, Ebele provided a solution to a dispute that arose among two groups in the town, suggesting that one of the groups had to leave the town. After settling the dispute, he was made the chief of the town.

Funzi (Mfunzi) Fjort, Republic of Congo

Funzi or Mfuzi is a myth about a blacksmith of the Fjort people of Congo. His story shows that after the river god gave the Fjort people fire, Funzi was the one that taught them how to work using iron and copper. The Fjort people also acknowledge Funzi as the one who created lightning in that while he hit his hammer on his anvil, sparks came forth from it.

Chapter 2

Differences between areas and cultures inside africa (ex. immigration, slave trade, colonialism, etc.)

Egypt

Egypt is a country in the Northeastern part of Africa, originally known as the United Arab Republic. The official language in the country is Arabic since the 7th century; *Masri* is the Egyptian Arabic dialect of the people.

Egypt is at the center of the foundation of African history. Proof of ancient civilization in Egypt (Egyptian empire) has been found to be in existence between 2600 to 30 BC.

Slave trade

People from the Oases, as well as Upper Egypt, were the main Slave traders in Egypt. Other major slave traders were the Bedouin people and villagers from Buhayra province. The traders were divided into groups of black slave traders and white slave traders, and they had an association. The greatest slave depot and front for the slave trade was Cairo. There was a yearly event for the trading of slaves called the mawlid of Ṭanṭā.

Colonization

French Domination of Egypt (1798–1882)

France was discovered to have invaded Egypt between the 17th and 18th centuries; however, the reason France finally landed in Egypt in the year 1798 under the leadership of Napoleon was that France was at war with Britain. Upon taking control, Napoleon did a lot to show that he supported Islam so as to gain the Egyptians' goodwill. During that time, animosity for foreign leadership grew among the Egyptians, and using barrage fire, they launched an unanticipated attack on the French.

Not long after, Napoleon faced defeat at the hands of Ottoman Syria when he tried to take control of Acre. This made him depart from Egypt, sneaking past the British fleet on the 22nd of August. The next French general in chief, Jean-Baptiste Kléber tried to take control of Egypt again. The Ottomans did the same; however, the French defeated them at Heliopolis. Soon after, Kléber was assassinated by a Syrian on the 14th of June.

The next person to take power was 'Abd Allāh Jacques Menou, and during his time (1801), Egypt was being invaded by the British forces from Abu Qīr, the Ottomans from Syria, and British Indian forces from Qusayr; French military surrendered in June at Cairo, and Menou surrendered in September at Alexandria. The British then established Dual Control over Egypt to rule besides khedives.

European Intervention

Egyptians took control of their country, and in the years 1805 to 1879, there were a lot of administrative changes; it was in 1879 that the Europeans began to rule over Egypt. Although Europe was in power, they ruled with apprehension.

British Domination (1882–1956)

Development in Egypt really kicked in when the British took authority over Egypt. The British government was liberal and reluctant because it seemed that establishing a formal political authority would result in a revolt from the sultan and other European powers. Though the British had to secure their interests, and that called for the presence of the military.

British protectorate over Egypt did not last because of the Unilateral Declaration of Egyptian Independence on the 28th of February 1992. A little later, Sultan Fuad declared himself King of Egypt even though the brits still occupied Egypt. Brits began to send forces to defend the Suez Canal following the Anglo-Egyptian treaty of 1936 as well as train Egypt's Army. In 1956, a coup d'état forced the brits to pull back their forces, and in the same year, Britain warred against Egypt over domination of the Suez Canal, but they lost.

Immigration

The first immigrants into Egypt were the Turkish, who departed from Central Asia. They arrived in a country that was home to one of the earliest civilizations of the world and who also contributed a great deal to the history of Islam due to their understanding of administration, military control, and very active culture. As a result of the occupancy of the Turks in Egypt, the Tulunid dynasty featured a series of Egyptian leaders who were either originally Turks or they were brought up in accordance with the norms of Turkish culture and state.

Although there are no records of any historical immigration into Egypt by the Turkish, a lot of Turks arrived at and occupied lands in the country. There are those who took place as their new home while others stayed for a period of time, and then they departed. Among the Egyptian immigrants from Turkey, some came to search for riches and better conditions of living while some came for official purposes, and others for the purpose of studying.

When the Turks were on the verge of losing the Ottoman Empire to Europe, its army arrived in Egypt under the leadership of Muhammad Ali' Pasha, and Muhammad Ali' took over the leadership of Egypt in 1805 up until 1952.

Legends

Legend of Creation

Heka is a force that existed before creation, which empowered the gods and is responsible for every aspect of life. Atum (Ptah) was a god that rose up and then gave birth to Shu (god of air), who gave the principles of life to the early world, and Tefnut (goddess of moisture), who contributed to the principles of order. Tears from Atum's 'All seeing eye' also birthed men and women. Shu and Tefnut gave birth to Geb (earth) and Nut (sky). Geb and Nut birthed Osiris, Isis, Set, Nephthys, and Horus.

Osiris emphasized *ma'at* (harmony) while ruling the world with his sister/wife, Isis but Set envied his power and glory. Set cut Osiris in 42 pieces and scattered the parts all over Egypt. Isis was in despair at Osiris's death and with the loss of his body, and immediately, she and Nephthys set out to find the parts. Upon finding a body part, they built a shrine to shield it from Set, and this gave birth to the 42 Egyptian provinces. When they gathered all the parts, Isis assembled Osiris and mated with him to give birth to Horus, after which Osiris went to the underworld, where he became the ruler of the dead. When Horus, Osiris's son, grew up, he challenged his uncle Set to battle, and Set was defeated.

Egyptians believe that after death, a person's soul appears before the Hall of Truth before Osiris for judgment. The white feather of ma'at is weighed against the person's heart; if the heart is lighter, it is allowed passage into the Field of Reeds (eternal bliss), if the heart is heavier, the soul is consumed by Ammut (gobbler) and ceases to exist.

Legend of Apophis

Another legend is that of Apophis, an evil creature resembling a dragon skull on the horizon and every evening. When the sun passes through the underworld, Apophis attempted to stop it. A clear sky meant the sun passed easily. A blood-red sun indicated a battle between good and evil, which left the sun victorious and meant new dawn.

Nigeria

Nigeria, officially known as the Federal Republic of Nigeria, is located in West Africa, having 36 states, and is home to ancient and indigenous pre-colonial states and kingdoms.

Slave trade

When the transatlantic slave trade commenced, slaves were supplied from the southeastern part of Nigeria to European slave traders by traditional slave traders. Despite the official ban placed on the slave trade by the British administration in the middle of the 1800s, it still continued silently up until the 1930s and was finally put to an end in the 1940s.

About 3000 people were taken as slaves from West Africa every year before the year 1650, and in the final quarter of that century, the number of slaves that left West Africa was 20,000 a year. Slave trade was worse between the years 1700 and 1850 – in those years, an average of about 76,000 people were taken from Africa between 1783 and 1792. When it first started, the trading of slaves was usually done in West Central Africa, now known as the Congo. The front for the sale of slaves moved to the Bight of Benin in the 1700s, and it came to be called the Slave Coast. The major ports on the coast for transporting slaves abroad were Ouidah (which is now a part of Benin) and Lagos. In Lagos alone, the number of slaves that were bought was about 2,000 between the years 1790 and 1807, although mostly by the British, but later, the Portuguese took over and started buying. In 1740, the main slave traffickers in the Bight of Biafra were the British – the ports in the Bight of Biafra include Old Calabar (Akwa Akpa), Bonny, and New Calabar. In 1767, the British made it easy for dozens of people to be murdered at Calabar after they had invited those people to their ships – the brits did this apparently to settle a local quarrel.

In the year 1807, the Slave Trade Act was enacted by the Parliament of the United Kingdom, which barred the British from partaking in the slave trade. When Britain ceased from partaking in the slave trade, it constituted a major decrease in the transportation of slaves to North, South, and Central America, and this decrease in the slave trade was what led to the collapse of the Edo Empire because it was the major slave-trading state. The French and the British bought more slaves from Edo ports than other European powers.

Lagos became one of the major slave ports in the late 1700s up to the 1850s. Most of the slave-trading done during that period was illegal, and as a result, there isn't much data to give the actual estimate of how many slaves were bought. However, the Trans-Atlantic Slave Voyage Database shows that 308,800 slaves were transported from Lagos across the Atlantic between the years 1776 and 1850. The French and the British were the most involved in the business of trading slaves until 1807 when the Spanish and Portuguese stepped in. Between the years 1826 and 1850, the Royal Navy of Britain started interfering with the trading of slaves from Lagos.

African and European historians continue to argue to this day whether the British colonized Nigeria because their motives were a benevolence toward putting a stop to slavery or because they just wanted to demonstrate their wealth and power. But the fact remains that slavery and its effects had already wiped out most of the Nigerian population to the point that there was chaos, which called for the enforcing of colonization.

Colonization

West Africa was under the rule of the British in the middle of the 19th century, and so, Great Britain colonized Nigeria. After the slave trade was prohibited, the brits occupied Lagos in 1861 and established the Oil River Protectorate in 1884.

Between 1886 and 1899, the majority of Nigeria was under the governorship of George Taubman Goldie of the Royal Niger Company. The control of the Protectorates of Northern and Southern Nigeria was taken over by the British government in 1900, and in 1906, the Lagos colony was merged with the Protectorate of Southern Nigeria.

The administration of the Protectorates was centrally under the Colonial Civil Service, which had Residents and District officers that were appointed over each region. Each region had a Native Administration led by District Heads and traditional rulers (Emirs in the north, and Obas in the south).

Sir Frederick Lord Lugard kept pushing for the entire Nigerian territory to be unified, and it wasn't till August 1911 that the Colonial Office asked him to lead the amalgamated colony. Lugard came back to Nigeria after his 6-year term as Governor of Hong Kong to supervise the merging of the northern and southern protectorates in 1912. On the 9th of May, 1913, he submitted an official proposal for both the northern and southern provinces to have separate administrations but remained under the control of the office of the Governor-General. The Colonial Office accepted most of Lugard's plans, but the idea of him being in control and making decisions without their consent didn't sit well with them.

Regardless, the northern and southern protectorates of Nigeria were officially unified and became one colony and protectorate under the control of the proconsul with the title 'Governor-General of Nigeria' in the year 1914. After uniting the northern and southern protectorates, the British employed the system of indirect rule to preside over the northern and southern regions.

The system of indirect rule where the structure of authority was focused on the emir did not bring about change in the north. While the emirs were very comfortable with their roles as dependable agents of indirect rule, the colonial masters did not do much; rather, they thought it best to leave things as they were, especially when it came to religion. Christian missionaries were not permitted in the north, and the little efforts made by the government towards educating the young were combined with Islamic institutes.

In the south, however, traditional rulers were a medium for the indirect rule in Edo and Yoruba lands except that the priestly functions of the rulers were weakened by Christianity and Western education. This called for dual loyalty; first, to the view of sacred rulership because of the symbolical value it held, and second, to the modern conception of law and governance. Because of the respect that was awarded to traditional rulership, the Oba of Benin, whose office lay with Edo religious belief, was allowed to assume sponsorship of a political movement of the Yorubas. While in the Eastern Region, the people did not accept the leadership of certain officials who were appointed and given 'warrants' – which led to the rise of the nomenclature known as 'warrant chiefs' – because they did not have any original traditional claims.

Uniting the Northern Nigerian Protectorate with the Southern Nigerian Protectorate entailed that there would be an informal relationship between three different subdivisions of regional governing bodies in Nigeria: the Northern, Eastern, and Western regions. Each of these regions had independent government roles and were ruled by a Lieutenant Governor who supervised almost all independent units whose economic interests coincided but had uncommon social and political interests. The colonial government was very careful not to do anything that was in violation of Islam so as to prevent any challenges that may step on traditional northern values and ultimately lead to opposition to British rule.

The process of governance with the system of an indirect rule meant that the local rulers had to interact with the colonial officials at all times, and the system was designed in such a way as to accommodate all the regions. For example, the rule of law was a decree that was signed by the emir and the Governor in the north, whereas, in the south, the Governor had to consult with the Legislative Council before making any legislative decisions. The recognized official language in the north was Hausa, and the colonial officials were required to know and understand it. The English language was the recognized language in the south. Differences in Regional administration was also recognized in the quality of the personnel appointed to every local region as well as the range of operations that they were capable of handling. The British staff in all three regions continued their operations in the same way as had been before the northern and southern protectorates were united.

F. Lugard submitted another proposal to the Colonial Office, which granted the Governor the liberty of not staying in the country on a full-time basis, and the proposal was accepted. As a result, for four months out of the year, Lord Lugard took stayed in London. However, a good number of the persons involved found it to be baffling, so they disapproved of it, and with time, the practice was terminated.

In the year 1916, F. Lugard created a body comprised of six traditional rulers that included the Sultan of Sokoto, Emir of Kano, and Oba of Benin to represent all the parts of the colony; the body was called the Nigerian Council. This council was a supposed means for members to express their opinions so as to give the Governor-General an idea of how to preside over the amalgamated state. However, during the meetings, F. Lugard only informed the traditional rulers about British policy, and all the leaders could do was to pay attention and concur.

Lugard kept trying to solidify the sovereignty of the British and ensuring local governance through traditional rulership. He disliked the fact that most of the educated and Westernized Nigerians were in the south, which is why he suggested that the country's capital be moved to Kaduna (the north) from Lagos, but the capital was never moved. F. Lugard passed down his authority as Governor-General to his successor in the year 1918 when his tenure ended.

Immigration

Immigrants into Nigeria were mostly from other African countries, especially West African nations. Statistics show that immigrants in Nigeria are from countries such as Ghana, Benin, Mali, Chad, and Niger. Most of the immigrants in Nigeria are Liberians.

Legends

Bayajida

This tale talks about a man that landed in Daura. He was a warrior by the name Bayajida. On reaching Daura, he wanted to drink water; he was told that a snake was living in the only well in the town, and the only way to draw water was when there were more people capable of holding down the snake. Bayajida went to the well alone, and while drawing water, the snake clung to the rope that was attached to the bucket for drawing the water. Seeing the snake, he caught it by the head with his left hand and used his sword to cut off the head. He placed it in his satchel and left.

When the queen of the town saw that the snake was dead, she promised half the town to the person who killed the snake. Many claimed to have killed the snake but were unable to provide proof. At this, Bayajida stepped up and showed the queen the snake's head. Queen Daurama offered him half the town, but he asked for her hand in marriage instead.

Shango

Shango (Sango) is the god of thunder and lightning, according to the Yorubas, who lives in the sky. He had three wives called *orisas,* meaning goddesses; Oya, who was the goddess of the river Niger, Oshun (Osun), who was the goddess of Osun river, and Obba (Oba), who was the goddess of the Oba river.

Shango is usually represented with two axes, which is the symbol of thunderbolt on either his head, his six eyes, and sometimes three heads. Sometimes he is represented with a ram, whose bellows sounds like thunder. His servants were Afefe (wind) and Oshumare (rainbow).

South Africa

South Africa is officially called the Republic of South Africa (RSA). It has three capital cities; Pretoria is the executive, Bloemfontein is the judicial, and Cape Town is the legislative. The largest city in South Africa is Johannesburg.

Slave trade

Jan van Riebeek, founder of the first Cape Colony in 1652, initially tried to negotiate for cattle and human labor. However, when the negotiations were dropped, the British then opted for slavery. A total of 250 slaves were first imported into South Africa in 1658, out of which only 170 made the journey. Slave traders from Ghana also sent 228 slaves to the Cape on the 6th of May 1658. From the year 1710, the population of adult slaves was three times more than the population of adult colonials.

The fleet of the VOC returning from Batavia and other eastern areas also carried slaves; slave trade was not legal in the Netherlands so the slaves could not be sent to Europe. As a result of this, the slaves were sold at better prices at the Cape than in the East Indies.

Colonization

Dutch Colonization

After the Cape sea route was discovered in the year 1652, Jan van Riebeeck set up a virtual station at the Cape of Good Hope, which is now known as the Cape Town, on behalf of the Dutch East India Company. Sometime later, the Cape of Good Hope turned into a place for an enormous population of vrijlieden or as they are also called, vrijburges meaning 'free citizens' – these are people who used to work for the Dutch

East India Company and decided to stay in Dutch territories abroad after their contracts had been served. Dutch traders also brought a lot of slaves from Indonesia, Madagascar, and some areas of Eastern Africa into the Cape. The mixed-race communities that were formed came about through unions between vrijburgers, their slaves, and some indigenes. The Cape Coloureds is one such communities that was formed, and as a result, most of these people took up the Dutch language and Christianity.

When the Dutch tried to expand toward the east, it resulted in a lot of wars with the Xhosa tribe emerging from the southwest – these wars were later famed Xhosa Wars. Each side was competing for land near the Great Fish River upon which they could graze their cattle. Some vrijburgers who turned out to be independent farmers on the frontier were called Boers, and those among them who adopted quasi-nomadic modus vivendi were known as trekboers. The Boers created military reserves, which they called commandos and allied themselves with the Khoisan groups in order to force Xhosa raids back. The opposing sides continued to launch violent attacks on each other, and combined with this, there was a theft of farm animals for many decades.

British Colonization

Cape Town was taken over by the British between the years 1795 and 1803 so that the French First Republic that had invaded the 'Low Countries' wouldn't. Although the Cape fell back under Dutch rule under the Batavian Republic in 1803, in 1806, the British assumed control again. When the Napoleonic Wars ended, the Cape was formally given over to the British, and it became an essential part of the British Empire. The British started migrating to South Africa in 1818, and that was what brought about the coming of the 1820 settlers. The new settlers were allowed to settle for a number of reasons, which includes growing the European workforce as well as strengthening the regions around the frontier against any attacks from Xhosa.

The first twenty years of the 19th century featured a powerful Zulu people who, under their leader, Shaka kept expanding their territories. In the early 1820s, the wars that Shaka started indirectly caused the Mfecane – crushing – where about 2 million people lost their lives, which resulted in the desolation and depopulation of the inland plateau. The Matabele people (a branch of the Zulu) under the leadership of king Mzilikazi created a larger empire that comprised the highveld.

A lot of Dutch colonists left the Cape Colony in a sequence of migratory groups that were later known as Voortrekkers – meaning 'Pathfinders' or 'Pioneers' – in the 1800s because they didn't like being subservient to the Brits. The settlers journeyed to the future Natal, Free State, and Transvaal regions. The Boers became founders of the Boer Republics made up of the South African Republic (Gauteng, Limpopo, Mpumalanga, and the North West provinces), the Natalia Republic (KwaZulu-Natal), and the Orange Free State (Free State).

President Thomas François Burgers of the South African Republic (Transvaal) proclaimed war against Sekhukhune and the Pedi on the 16th of May 1876, but he was defeated on the 1st of Augu[st] 1876. On the 16th of February 1877, a peace treaty was signed between them at Botshabel, and Paul Kruger took over after Burgers left because he failed to conquer Sekhukhune. The Brits, led by the secretary for native affairs of Natal, Theophilus Shepstone, then took over the South African Republic (Transvaal) on the 12th of April 1877. The British also tried and failed to subdue Sekhukhune in 1878 and 1879 until November 1879 when Sir Garnet Wolseley attacked with 2,000 British soldiers, Boers, and 10,000 Swazis.

Immigration

Immigrants into South Africa from Europe arrived in the country between the middle and the latter part of the 17th century. They were people from the Netherlands, France, Great Britain, Germany, and Ireland. Later in the 20th century, more Europeans arrived in the country, mostly in search of better living conditions. In the middle of the 1970s, Portuguese departed from the colonies of Portugal in Southern Africa, such as Angola and Mozambique, after the colonies gained their independence and migrated to South Africa.

Legends

Captain Van Hunks

In the 18th century, according to legend, a sea captain, Jan Van Hunks retired to live on Table Mountain with his wife. Every day he went up the mountain to smoke his pipe and to see the view. One day he went up, and to his surprise, a man was already there; the man challenged him to a smoking contest, and Van Hunks won. The strange man was actually the devil who took Van Hunks with him because he lost.

The thick cloud hanging above Table Mountain today is believed to remain from the smoking contest.

Two Roads overcame the Hyena.

A hungry hyena saw a fork that split into two paths, each of which led to two goats caught in thickets. The Hyena couldn't decide between the two paths and decided to walk down the left path with its left leg and the right path with its right leg. The paths grew further, and the Hyena was eventually split into two halves.

This encourages people to choose a single path and be dedicated to it, or they will be stretched too thin.

Chapter 3

The story of ancient Africa at the dawn

Before the arrival of the Europeans in Africa, the human settlements in the continent were largely made up of primitive people. The major occupations were farming (growing crops and rearing of animals for food), hunting. The clothing at that time was usually a piece of cloth or leather that was worn in between the legs. The ends of which were inserted into a string that runs around the waist meant only to cover the genitals. Bracelets were worn on the wrists and arms to complete this mode of dressing. The men frequently carried bows and arrows, javelins, and axes with which they armed themselves.

Central Africa

Sao Civilization

Beginning from the 6th century BC and onward to the 16th century AD, Sao Civilization in Central Africa was very prosperous. South of the Lake Chad, by the Chari River, is a territory that is presently part of Cameroon, and Chad was where the Sao people lived. This civilization is the most formal civilization whose existence in the Cameroonian territory can't be in doubt since they left apparent hints regarding their existence.

There are many ethnic groups of southern Chad and northern Cameroon who say that they are descendants of the Sao civilization, and chiefly among these ethnic groups with such claims is the Sara people. Artifacts left behind by Sao people show that they were people who worked with their hands crafting bronze, copper, and iron items. Some of the findings gotten from this civilization are bronze sculptures, terracotta statues of humans and animals, coins, funeral urns, household utensils, jewelry, highly decorated pottery, and spears.

Kanem Empire

The Chad Basin was the center of the Kanem empire. Kanem Empire was the name given to this empire beginning in the 9th century AD down till 1893 when it became the independent kingdom of Bornu.

The empire had a large landmass covering the majority of Chad, some areas of present-day southern Libya, eastern Niger, northeastern Nigeria, northern Cameroon, some areas of the Central African Republic, and South Sudan. The rise of the Kanem Empire began in the 8th century in the north and east area of Lake Chad. Sometime in the 9th century AD, the Kanem Central Sudanic Empire was established at Njimi by the rovers whose language was Kanuri – their trading was centered on getting horses from North Africa and providing slaves in exchange. In the 11th century, the Islamic Sayfawa (Saifawa) dynasty was established by Humai (Hummay) ibn Salamna.

The dynasty of Sayfawa was in power for a period of over seven (7) centuries and was, therefore, one of the dynasties that have lasted longest in the history of human civilizations. Another major source of income for the empire was a tax imposed on local farms. The land of the empire was said to be large enough to contain a cavalry of 40,000, extending from Fezzan in the north and Sao state in the south. Islam was the main religion, and most of its citizens were frequent pilgrims to Mecca so much that Cairo had special hostels for Kanem pilgrims. The shrinking decline, and ultimate defeat of this great empire occurred in the 14th century when Bilala encroachers from the area around Lake Fitri attacked.

Borno Empire

In the 18th century, Bornu became a place where Islamic education was centered on. The empire once had a great army, but by failing to import more novel weapons, the army soon lost recognition, and the decline of Kamembu had started at that time. Drought and famine had been growing immensely as well as the internal rebellion in the pastoralist north, growth of Hausa power, and importation of small arms responsible for the extreme bloodshed weakened the *Mai's* (ruler) power. The last *Mai* was overthrown in 1841, and that brought the Sayfawa Dynasty to an end; in its place, the al-Kanemi Dynasty of the *Shehu* assumed rulership.

Shilluk Kingdom

The Shilluk Kingdom was established in the middle of the 15th century AD by Nyikang, its first monarch. South Sudan was where the Shilluk Kingdom was centered in the 15th century along with a long piece of land by the western bank of the White Nile, and at about 12^0 N from Lake No. Fashoda was the name of the town where the capital and royal residence of the kingdom were sited.

Baguirmi Kingdom

During the 16th and 17th centuries, the Baguirmi Kingdom stood as an independent state southeast of the Lake Chad, which is the present-day country of Chad. The kingdom came out toward the southeast of the Kanem-Bornu Empire. The first ruler of the kingdom was Mbang Birni Besse, and it was while he was still in power that the kingdom was subdued by Bornu and transformed into an affluent.

Wadai Empire

Wadai Kingdom was established by the Tunjur people to the east of Bornu in the 16th century, and in the 17th century, the center of the kingdom was positioned on Chad and the Central African Republic. It was also in the 17th century that the Maba people began its rebellion and established the Muslim dynasty. Originally, the Wadai Kingdom was a tributary of Bornu and Durfur; however, it became an independent kingdom and great opposition to the neighboring kingdoms.

Luba Empire

Around 1300 and 1400 AD, a member of the Balopwe clan by the name of Kongolo Mwamba (Nkongolo) united all the Luba people near Lake Kisale into one. He also established the Kongolo Dynasty that was eventually booted out by Kalala Ilunga. Ilunga then spread the kingdom out towards the west of Lake Kisale. Later on, a central political system of spiritual kings (*balopwe*) ruled in conjunction with a court council of head governors and sub-heads all the way to village heads. The political system of the Luba people later spread through Central Africa, southern Uganda, Rwanda, Burundi Malawi, Zambia, Zimbabwe, and western Congo. The *balopwe* were chosen by ancestral spirits, and so they had direct contact with the spirits and communicated with them. States that were merged into the political system and with their titles could be represented in court. The spiritual power of the *balopwe* was where their authorities lay. Not their military authority besides the army wasn't that large. The

Luba was capable of collecting tribute, which they redistributed, as well as oversee regional trade. Many states branched out from the kingdom, and the founders of these states claimed that they are descendants of the Luba. The major empires that claimed to be descendants of the Luba are the Lunda Empire and Maravi empire; northern Zambia people (the Bemba and Basimba) are descendants of the Luba immigrants into Zambia in the 17th century.

Lunda Empire

A Luba from the Ilunga Tshibinda royal family got married to Rweej, the queen of Lunda, and unified all the people of Lunda in the year 1450. The kingdom was then expanded by *mulopwe* Luseeng. Further expansion of the Lunda Empire was carried out by Luseeng's son, Naweej, who later became known as the first emperor of the empire, and his title was *mwato yamvo* (*mwaant yaav*, *mwant yav*) meaning the Lord of Vipers. The empire continued with the political system of the Luba, and it integrated into the system the people it had subdued. A *ciool* or *kilolo* (royal adviser) and the tax collector were delegated to each subdued state by the *mwato yamvo*.

There are a lot of states who claim that they are descendants of Lunda. For instance, the Imbangala people of inland Angola claim that they are descended from the brother of Queen Rweej, Kinguri, who could not bear being under the rule of *mulopwe* Tshibunda. As such, kings of states who were founded by the brother of Queen Rweej were called *Kinguri*. The Luena (Lwena) and Lozi (Luyani) of Zambia claim that they are also Kinguri's descendants. In the 17th century, chief and warrior of Lunda by the name of Mwata Kazembe created in the valley of Luapula River, an eastern kingdom of the Lunda. Expansion of the Lunda to the west was what gave rise to claims by the Yaka and Pende that they are also descendants. Lunda empire was united into Central

Africa with the coming of the western coast trade. The 19th century saw the last of the Lunda kingdom when the Chokwe invaded with guns as weapons.

Kingdom of Kongo

As in the 15th century AD, the Bakongo people, who were mostly farmers, were united together to form the Kingdom of Kongo under the leadership of their ruler named *manikongo,* whose dwelling place was the area of Pool Malebo, lower Congo River. The capital of the kingdom was M'banza-Kongo. Due to the fact that they were more organized than their neighbors, they subdued and turned their neighbors into tributaries. They possessed great metalwork skills as well as pottery and raffia cloth weaving. They encouraged trade between regions through a tribute system that was under the control of the *manikongo*. In the 16th century, the authority of the *manikongo* spanned through the Atlantic, which was west to Kwango River in the east. A *mani-mpembe* was delegated to all the territories under the kingdom.

Northeastern Africa (Horn of Africa)

Somalia

Islam was birthed directly across the Somalia Red Sea coast, and they traded with Arab Muslims. This was why merchants and sailors of Somalia that lived on the Arabian Peninsula were steadily influenced by the religion. As Muslim families migrated from the world of Islam to Somalia in the early Islamic centuries, followed by the conversion of the people of Somalia to the religion due to the aid of the Somalian Muslim scholars centuries after, the old city-states transformed into Islamic Mogadishu, Berbera, Zeila, Barawa and Merka who were a part of the ancestors of modern Somalians known as the Berber civilization. Mogadishu was later known as the City of Islam, and it presided over the trading of gold in East Africa for many centuries.

Ethiopia

Zagwe Dynasty commanded authority over many areas of what is today known as Ethiopia and Eritrea between 1137 and 1270. 'Zagwe' is gotten from northern Ethiopia, precisely the Cushitic speaking Agaw. As of 1270 AD, Solomonic Dynasty took over the rulership of the Ethiopian Empire, and this continued for several centuries.

North Africa

Maghreb (Maghrib)

As of 711 AD, North Africa had been subdued by the Umayyad Caliphate, and so in the 10th century, most of the North African population were Muslims. As of 9th century AD, an end was put to the conquest of North Africa by Islam and its cultures. Although the Umayyads presided over the Caliphate, having their capital in Damascus, the Abbasids soon took over, and the capital was transferred to Baghdad. The people of Berber, however, who due to a rejection of foreign powers meddling in their dealings, adopted Shi'ite and Kharijite Islam, which was considered antagonistic to the Abbasids. A lot of Kharijite empires arose and were cut down within the 8th and 9th centuries while declaring independence from Baghdad. In the early 10th century, Syrian Shi'ite groups created the Fatimid Dynasty in Maghreb, conquering the whole of Maghreb in 950 AD and the whole of Egypt in 969 AD, thus cutting themselves off from Baghdad. In the year 1050, ¼ a million Arabs departed Egypt for Maghreb.

Sudan

People who are connected with the site of Ballana moved to Nubia from the southwest and created three kingdoms – Makuria, Nobadia, and Alodia – after Meroe was dismissed by Ezana of Aksum. Makuria stood across the 3rd Cataract toward the Dongola Reach, and its capital was located at Dongola. Nobadia was toward the north of the 3rd Cataract, and its capital was Faras; toward the south of the 3rd Cataract was Alodia with Soba as its capital. Later, Nobadia was annexed into Makuria.

Egypt

Rashidun Caliphate took over Byzantine Egypt in 642 AD. Normally, under the Fatimid Caliphate, there was prosperity in Egypt – there was an increase in the production of wheat, barley, flax, and cotton, and the dams and canals were fixed. Clothes made from linen and cotton became majorly produced by Egypt, which led to an increase in the country's trade in the Mediterranean and the Red Sea. Egypt even issued a gold currency by the name of Fatimid dinar, which came to be used for trading with foreign nations. Most of the nation's income was generated from taxes.

Egyptians, before the coming of Europeans, had a monarchy that they believed was divine.

Southern Africa

Great Zimbabwe and Mapungwe

The first state in Southern Africa was the Mapungubwe Kingdom, which came up in the 12th century CE and had its capital located at Mapungubwe. The kingdom attained wealth by directing the trade of ivory from the Limpopo Valley, copper from the mountains of northern Transvaal, and gold from the Zimbabwe Plateau located between Limpopo and Zambezi rivers.

Following the waning of the Kingdom of Mapungubwe arose Great Zimbabwe on the Zimbabwe Plateau. Great Zimbabwe turned out to be the first city in Southern Africa, and an empire was centered upon it. The people of Great Zimbabwe were builders, a skill that was passed down from Mapungubwe – they built the wall of the Great Enclosure. Great Zimbabwe was a major source of gold, and trade with Swahili Kilwa, and Sofala was what helped it to thrive.

Namibia

Most states in Southern African were already established as of 1500 AD. The Ovambo in northwestern Namibia were farmers by occupation while the Herero were herders. With the increase in the number of cattle, the Herero moved toward the south to central Namibia to get access to better land for grazing. The Ovambanderu expanded to Ghanzi in northwestern Botswana. The Nama people who raised sheep and spoke Khoi moved up north till they met with the Herero; the struggle for land led to conflict between them.

South Africa and Botswana

Sotho-Tswana

Sotho-Tswana states began to develop toward the south of the Limpopo River in 1000 CE. The power of the chief of these people was determined by how much cattle he had and the connection he had with the ancestors. The power residing within cattle numbers stood till around 1300 AD. Various people of these states were linked to the Indian Ocean through the Limpopo River.

Nguni Land

One great period of disorderliness in southern Africa was *Mfecane* meaning 'the crushing', which was initiated by northern Nguni kingdoms, which include Mthethwa, Ndwandwe, and Swaziland because resources were scarce and there was famine. After the death of Dingiswavo of Mthethwa, Shaka took over. Shaka was a member of the Zulu people, he established the Zulu Kingdom, and he used his powers to rule over the Ndwandwe and moved the Swazi up north; when Ndwandwe and Swazi scattered, it led to the dissemination of Mfecane. Shaka extended the kingdom so much that the kingdom had tributaries coming from deep in the south – the rivers of Tugela and Umzimkulu. Shaka was killed by his half-brother Dinganne in 1828.

Khoisan and Boers

People were integrated into the Bantu people like Sotho and Nguni when Bantu was expanded. However, that ended because of the winter rainfall in the region. Khoisan people had trade exchanges of products like cattle, sheep and hunted game with the Bantu people for copper, tobacco, and iron.

Southeast Africa

Swahili Coast

The interaction with Muslim Arab and Persian traders led to the development of the mixed Arab, Persian, and African Swahili city-states, and the Swahili culture that emanated from these interactions show influences of the Arabs and Islam that had not been experienced in Bantu culture. The Bantu people of earlier times that occupied the Southeast coast of modern-day Kenya and Tanzania, who came across settlers from Persia and Arabia, acknowledged the trading settlements of Azania, Menouthias, and Rhapta; this is what eventually led to the derivation of the name, Tanzania.

According to history, far up north as northern Kenya and deep down south as Ruvuma River in Mozambique are places you can find Swahili people.

Urewe

Urewe culture was widely spread through the region of Lake Victoria in the African Iron Age. Artifacts of the people of this culture can be found in the Kagera Region of Tanzania, the Kivu region of the Democratic Republic of Congo down to the Nyanza and the Western provinces of Kenya. The culture of the Urewe people goes far back as the 5th century up to the 6th century AD, and the culture's origin emanates from the Bantu expansion from Cameroon.

Madagascar and Merina

Settlers from Southeast Asia who speak Austronesian were the first to land in Madagascar before the 6th century AD, followed by the Bantu people from the East African mainland during the 6th or 7th century. Cultivation of rice and bananas was brought in by the Austronesian speakers, while cattle rearing and other forms of farming were brought in by the

Bantu. Islam was introduced to Madagascar during the 14th century, and during the Middle Ages of East Africa, Madagascar was functioning as a port where Swahili seaport city-states like Sofala, Kilwa, Mombasa, and Zanzibar came in contact. Just past the 15th century, the emergence of kingdoms like the Sakalava Kingdom, Tsitambala Kingdom, and Merina began, and during the 19th century, the whole of Madagascar was under Merina control.

Lake Plateau states and empires

Kitara and Bunyoro

In 1000 AD, a lot of states emerged on the Lake Plateau from amongst the Great Lakes of East Africa. These states were into the cultivation of bananas, herding cattle, and cultivating cereals. The Bunyoro Kingdom is one of these first states (a part of the Kitara Empire). It ruled the entire region of the Great Lakes. This was a society whose culture was Nyoro at its core.

Buganda

Kato Kimera founded the Kingdom of Bugunda in the 14th century AD. The kingdom was under the rulership of the *kabaka* and clan heads known as the *Bataka*. After a period of time, the powers of the *Bataka* were reduced by the *kabakas* as Bugunda aimed at achieving an empire with a central authority. In the 16th century, Bugunda was trying to expand its lands, but it was rivaled by Bunyoro. Bugunda later in the 1870s became a very rich nation-state under the rulership of the *kabaka* and the then existing *Lukiko* – council of ministers. Not too long after, Bunyoro was conquered by Bugunda.

Rwanda

The Rwanda Kingdom was established somewhere around the 17th century at the bottom part of the western rift, near Lake Kivu. The elite groups of the kingdom were made up of bucolic Tutsi (BaTutsi), including the king known as *mwami*. The other group known as the Hutu (BaHutu) were farmers, and although they spoke one language with the Tutsi, certain stringent social standards did not allow them to interact or even marry. As oral tradition espouses, *Mwami* Ruganzu II –

Ruganzu Ndori founded the Kingdom of Rwanda between 1600 and 1624.

Burundi

The Kingdom of Burundi was founded by Tutsi chief Ntare Rushatsi and is located toward the south of the Kingdom of Rwanda. The bedrock upon which this kingdom was established includes cattle herding, cultivation by Hutu farmers, conquest, and politics.

Maravi

The Maravi people claim to have descended from Karonga (*kalonga*). They were the ones who linked Central Africa with Swahili Kilwa to the east coastal trade. The king of the Maravi people was called *karonga*. In the 17th century, the Maravi Kingdom had covered the area around Lake Malawi and the outskirts of the River Zambezi. *Karonga* Mzura tried to expand the kingdom; his death really impacted the empire, and it finally split in the 18th century.

West Africa

Sahelian empires and states

Ghana

As of the 8th century AD, the Ghana empire was founded by Dinge Cisse among the Soninke, and it became an established empire. The empire was made up of urban dwellers who were part of the empire's administrators and the rural farmers. Administrative power rested not only on urban dwellers whose religion was Islam, but also the *Ghana* (king) whose religious practice was traditional. There were two towns; the first was where the Muslim administrators, as well as the Berbers, lived, which had a pathway to the king's house paved with stone, while the other was the villages which were meant for rural dwellers that combined with larger societies who swore loyalty to the king. After subduing Aoudaghost, the empire converted to Islam, and by the 11th century, it began to wane.

Mali

Mali Empire was instituted in the 13th century AD following the defeat of the king of Sosso (southern Soninko), Soumaoro Kanté, by Sundiata (Lord Lion), who was the leader of Keita clan known as Mande (Mandingo) during the Battle of Kirina of the 12th century. After winning the war, Sundiata based the empire's capital at Niani. Despite their trading of salt and gold, a vital part of their economy was agriculture, and so was cattle, goat, sheep, and camel herding.

Songhai

Songhai people are the descendants of fishermen on the Middle Niger River with their capital based at Kukiya in the 9th century AD but was later moved to Gao around the 12th century. Songhai Empire was expanded to the north by Sonni Ali, and his move forced the Mossi closer toward the south of the Niger.

Songhai Empire was occupied by Morocco in 1951 under the rule of Ahmad al-Mansur of the Saadi Dynasty, and the aim was to possess the Sahel where gold could be mined. Djenne, Gao, and Timbuktu were captured by Morocco. However, they could occupy the entire Songhai region. In the 17th century, Songhai broke up into numerous states.

Sokoto Caliphate

The Fulani were always migrating, departing Mauritania, they formed settlements in Futa Tooro, Futa Djallon, and after some time, they were spread throughout West Africa. They converted to Islam in the 14th century CE, and they based themselves at Macina, southern Mali, by the 16th century. They declared jihads on non-Muslims in the 1670s, and many states were formed as a result of the jihad wars at Futa Tooro, Futa Djallon, Macina, Oualia, and Bundu. Among the states that were consequently formed was the Sokoto Caliphate, also called the Fulani Empire.

Forest empires and states

Akan kingdoms and the emergence of the Asante Empire

The language of the Akan people is Kwa. Many are of the opinion that people who speak Kwa originated from East/Central Africa prior to their settlement in the Sahel. The Akan Kingdom of Bonoman was established in the 12th century. When the mines of gold in present-day Mali began to dry, all the Akan states, including Bonoman, started to rise in the gold trading market. The Empire of Ashanti (Ashante) was heralded by Bonoman and other kingdoms Denkyira, Akyem, and Akwamu. During the 17th century, the people of Akan inhabited the state known as Kwaaman, located towards the north of Lake Bosomtwe. Its major source of revenue was derived from the trade of gold and kola nuts and forest clearing for the planting of yams. Ashanti Empire formed defense alliances with other kingdoms and became a tributary to Denkyira, Adansi, and Akwamu. The Ashante Empire stood for many years until it was destroyed by the British in 1900.

Dahomey

The Kingdom of Dahomey was established during the early period of the 17th century following the departure of the Aja people from the Allada kingdom to the north, where they took root among the Fon. By declaring their powers, a couple of years after their settlement, they created the Dahomey Kingdom, and the capital was located at Agbome. Between 1645 and 1685, king Houegbadia pronounced that every land in the kingdom would be owned by the king and should be taxed; he also turned the kingdom into a centralized state.

Yoruba

Yorubas thought of themselves as the people who lived in a United Kingdom. In 1000 AD, the first Yoruba city-state was founded and named Ile-Ife. Yorubas were ruled by an *Oba* with the *iwarefa* (council of chiefs) as his advisors. A loose confederacy of Yoruba city-states was created in the 18th century with Ife as the capital under the rulership of the Oni of Ife. During the 16th century, the Oyo Empire came up.

The Oyo Empire had a governing council, and for every region that the empire acquired, a local administrator was appointed to preside over it. Some of the productions of the Yoruba people include cloth, ironware, pottery, which was traded in exchange for salt, leather, and horses.

Benin

The Benin Empire had already been constituted in at mid-15th century. The empire sought to expand its borders and rule politically from early times. It was ruled by the *Oba* – meaning king – Ewuare between 1450 and 1480 AD, who, after strengthening central power, went to war against the neighboring kingdoms for 30 years. Benin expanded to reach Dahomey in the west, the Niger Delta in the east through the west African coast toward the Yoruba lands in the north, when he died.

The *Oba* got advice from the *uzama,* which was a council of chiefs and families with great power and influence, and town chiefs of different societal groups. After a period of time, the power of the *uzama* was weakened when administrative personnel was appointed. Furthermore, women were allowed to assume positions of authority. The queen's mother, for example, the mother of the oba of the future, had enormous power and influence.

Niger Delta and Igbo

Niger Delta in Nigeria is made up of many city-states that had diverse governments and were guarded by the delta waterways and thick vegetation. The city-states of the Niger Delta could be compared to the Swahili in East Africa. Places like Bonny, Kalabari, and Warri had kings; some such as Brass were republics that had small senates, while those in Cross River and Old Calabar were under the rulership of *ekpe* society traders.

The Igbo people resided towards the east of the delta while Aniomas, towards the west of the River Niger. In the 9th century, the Nri kingdom came up with its ruler called *Eze Nri*. It was a political unit that was comprised of independent and sovereign villages that had their own territories and names and were recognized by the towns and villages. The villages employed the majority rule (democracy) – its men, and sometimes women were included in the procedures for decision-making.

Chapter 4

Gods and goddesses from the African continent

Gods

1. Abassi

Abassi (Abasi) is the name given to the supreme god and creator among the Anang, Efik people of Nigeria who lived in the sky. He had two aspects to him; Abassi Onyong meaning 'the god above' and Abassi Isong, which means 'the god below.' Abassi created the world as well as the primeval man and woman, but he didn't want any competition, so he didn't permit them to live on earth, but his wife Atai disagreed, and Abassi was then forced to permit the primeval human couple to live on earth with the conditions that they refrain from reproducing or farming. The couple later went against the conditions and began tilling the ground as well as having children; this made Atai send death into the world. As a result, the couple died, and discord rose amongst the children.

2. Abradi

Abradi is the name given to the supreme god and creator among the Ama, Nyimang people of Sudan who lives in the sky. He is known to have unlimited power, which comes directly from him. People call on him in times of famine, drought, and epidemic. Once the sky was so close to the earth, women had to bend to cook; an annoyed woman stabbed the sky with a stirring rod, and this made Abradi angry so that he moved the sky far away from the earth.

Usually, when a person died, Abradi brought the person back to life the next day. However, a rabbit went to the people and told them to bury the dead man, or else Abradi would destroy them, and the people did so out of fear. Upon finding out, Abradi then declared that death would from thence be permanent.

3. Adroa

Adroa is of Lugbara, Democratic Republic of Congo, Sudan, and Ugandan origin. It is the name given to the supreme god and creator of all things. He had two aspects to him, just like many of the African gods; Adroa and Adro. Adroa was the sky god. He surpassed every limit of experience and knowledge of humans, which is why he stayed in the sky, and he was conceived of as *onyiru,* which means 'good.' It is said that Adroa created the primeval man whose name was Gborogboro and a primeval woman whose name was Meme (they were twins). Meme became the mother to all the animals. She also gave birth to male and female twin children. The aboriginal sets of twin children were not exactly humans in that they possessed superhuman abilities and magical powers, and they could do all sorts of amazing things. However, after many coevals that featured the birth of male and female twin children, Jaki and Dribidu, known as the hero ancestors, were born; their sons are believed to be the ones who established the modern-day Lugbara clans.

Adro was the god of the earth who existed and lived with humans and had the same limits as humans did; he was conceived of as *onzi,* which means 'bad.' His children were known as the Adroanzi. Furthermore, Adro was identified with death, and to gain his favor, humans had to use their children as a sacrifice. However, eventually, rams became the object of sacrifice instead of children.

4. Abgé

Abgé is of Fon origin in Benin Republic. Among all the Fon gods or deities known as Vodun, Abgé is among the chief of the Sea gods, which is one of the four gods into which Vodun was split into. He is the third son that was born to the Creator, Mawu-Lisa. He had a female twin sister by the name of Naètè, who was also his wife. At the time Mawu-Lisa split the various kingdoms of the universe amongst her children, she gave the sea to Abgé and Naètè to inhabit, and the command of the waters was given to them.

5. Agé

Agè is also of Fon origin in Benin Republic. He is a member of the Fon gods or deities (Vodun). Specifically, he is the god of the hunt and the fourth son born to Mawu-Lisa, the Creator. At the time Mawu-Lisa split the kingdoms of the universe amongst her children, she put Agè in charge of every land that was unoccupied and placed him in command of all game animals and birds.

6. Agipie

Agipie is of Turkana, the origin of Kenya. It is the name given to a god who had two different aspects to him that were at war with each other. The one aspect of Agipie was that of a good-hearted sky god, while the other aspect was that of a dangerous earth god that was identified with lightning and drowning. At whatever time, the two gods shot lightning bolts toward the other when fighting against each other, the result was the occurrence of a thunderstorm.

7. *Ajok*

Ajok, also known as Adyok or Naijok, is of Lotuko origin in Sudan. This is the name given to the supreme god and creator who in himself had a nature of benevolence; however, humans were required to constantly pray to him as well as offer up sacrifices, just so his good-hearted nature will be maintained. The Lotuko people tell a story of how death originated – it is said that a quarrel between a husband and his wife was what made Ajok angry to the point that he made death a lasting situation.

When the child of the man and woman was deceased, the mother pleaded with Ajok to restore her child's life, and Ajok did exactly that; however, when the husband found that his child was brought back to life, the husband was so furious that he lambasted his wife and killed the child. What ensued between the couple caused Ajok to make a decree to never bring any human back to life again, and from that moment on, death became a lasting and irreversible situation.

8. *kongoo*

Akongo is the supreme god of the Ngombe people in the Democratic Republic of Congo. He is known to have a close relationship with a human in the beginning, and he guarded and protected them. But with time, humans were given to quarreling, and when the quarrel amongst them grew severe, Akongo had to leave them and exiled himself to live in the forest, and since then, he was no longer seen or heard from.

9. *Amma*

Amma is the name given to the creator (god) people of the Dogon people of Mali and Burkina Faso. Some versions of the creation account of the Dogon people depict Amma as a male, while in some others, Amma is a female. The world and everything that exists within it was created by Amma; the earth was created when a lump of clay was projected into the heavens by this god. The sun and the moon were created when he took two earthenware bowls and shaped them, wrapping the bowl meant to be the sun in red copper while he wrapped the bowl meant to be the moon in white copper or brass. He then broke a piece of the sun, shattered the piece he broke, and threw the bits into space to form the stars. Another version states that he took pieces of clay and plunged them into the heavens. To the people of Dogon, the universe stands at the center of a world axis pillar known as Amma's House Post. This post also bears the sky, which the Dogon people believe is the roof of Amma's house.

10. Arebati

Aberati, also known as Arebate, Baatsi, and Tore amongst the Efe and Mbuti people of the Democratic Republic of Congo, is the supreme god and creator and god of the sky, but is also identified with the moon. Out of the 10 populations of Pygmies, the Efe and Mbuti are two. Some other groups of Pygmies believe Khonvoum to be the supreme god and creator instead of Arebati. In some groups, Aberati and Tore are the same, while other groups consider Aberati as the moon god while they view Tore as a god of forests and the hunt.

It is believed that the universe was created by Aberati as well as the primeval man who he formed from clay with the help of the moon; after Aberati had finished making the body of the man, he covered the clay with skin so as to bring the man to life. In the beginning, death was non-existent. Aberati made humans young again when they had grown old, and when a certain woman died, he restored her life. Aberati requested that a frog move the woman's body; however, a toad made a demand that he wanted to be the one to move the body, and Aberati permitted him. The toad was to sit with the body of the woman at the edge of a pit (symbolizing a grave) with a warning that neither of them (toad or woman) was to fall into the pit as there would be consequences. The toad fumbled, bashing the body of the woman into the pit, and he fell in as well. Based on the warning Aberati gave, there was a consequence as humans were doomed to die from that moment on.

A different myth tells that the supreme god known as Baatsi in the Efe story and Tore in the Mbuti myth told humans that they were free to eat the fruit of any tree except *tahu* and strict obedience to this rule awarded them the opportunity to live in the sky with Baatsi. A certain woman who was pregnant wanted to eat the *tahu* fruit so bad that she asked her husband to pick some for her. Dismayed by their disobedience, Baatsi sent death as a punishment.

11. Arum

Arum is the name given to the supreme god and creator among the Uduk people of Ethiopia, who is believed to have made everything that exists. The myth says that a great tree known as the *birapinya* tree connected the heavens with the earth; it reached the sky although the sky was closer to the earth than it is today, and humans, as well as the people living in the sky, used this tree as a means of conveyance between the earth and the heavens. The tree was cut down by a woman who thought she had been wronged, and so the conveyance was put to an end; the distance between the sky and the earth increased. Before the tree was cut down by the woman, death was not a lasting situation, but after the tree was cut down, it became permanent.

12. Asis

Asis, also called Asista, is the name given to the supreme god who created the sun, moon, sky, and earth among the

Kipsigis, Nandi people of Kenya. He is represented by the sun, and working through the sun, he created every creature of the earth from air, earth, and water. Next among his creation were the first four beings, which include a human, an elephant, a snake, and a cow. Despite being distant from humans, he provided them with all that was good and was the force underlying everything in the world. The spirits of the dead known as *oiik* were the mediators between humans and Asis, and whenever the balance of nature was disrupted by the humans, the *oiik* punished them.

13. Ataa Naa Nyongmo

Ataa Naa Nyongmo is the supreme god who created the world and everything that exists within it. He is usually identified with the sky. Ataa Naa Nyongmo was conceived of as a god that nurtures, which is typical of a cultural group that was into agriculture. He commanded rain, sunlight, and growth of crops. Whenever humans failed to properly perform their rites or went against his commands, he withheld the necessities of life from them as a punishment, or sometimes he caused the occurrence of destructive natural events like earthquakes.

14. Bumba

Bumba is the supreme god of the Bushongo people of the Democratic Republic of Congo. At the very beginning, there existed only water and darkness, and Bumba was alone. He had a stomachache and started to throw up; the first thing he spewed was the sun, and there was light, and the next thing he spewed was the moon and the stars. By vomiting again, Bumba brought out different animals, birds, and fish, and lastly, he chucked up humans. All the creatures he vomited were the foundation for other animals to be created; all the birds were created from a heron, lizards and other reptiles were created from a crocodile, all other insects were created from the beetle, and on it went. Bumba had three sons who completed the fashioning of the universe, and when all of it was done, it was given unto humans.

15. Chukwu

Chukwu, also known as Chi, is the supreme god and creator from whom all good came according to the Igbo people of Nigeria. He is also the head of all the gods of the Igbo people, and he had three aspects to him (a tercet); Chukwu, his foremost aspect means the great god; Chineke means the creative spirit, and Osebuluwa means the one who governs and directs everything. The sun was used to represent Chukwu. He commanded rainfall and the growth of plants. Just as is the case with a lot of African deities, Chukwu was originally living in the sky, and the sky was close to the earth so that humans could touch it. Because of the close proximity of the sky to the earth, a woman pounding her mortar with a pestle tended to hit the sky with the pestle, and when Chukwu requested that she should stop, she refused to listen, so he moved the sky far above the earth and was thus separated from his creations since that time.

When death came into the world in Igbo tradition, humans sent a dog to ask Chukwu to bring people who had died back to life; but a toad who caught the message and wanted to punish the people went ahead of the dog and told Chukwu that human didn't want to be restored to life after death. Chukwu agreed to this and was unable to change his mind even after the dog who had the accurate message arrived.

16. Deng

Deng or Denka (meaning) rain is a deity of rain and fecundity of the Dinka people of Sudan. He was the mediator that stood between humans and the supreme being, and sometimes he was either referred to as the son of God or as the son of the goddess Abuk. Deng and the supreme god Nhialic were close, and in some regions, they are seen as the same deity. A story of the origin of Deng includes myths that are nonconforming, telling stories of children who were born in an unconventional way and possessed supernatural abilities (powers).

A young lady who was pregnant appeared from the sky, and people welcomed with great esteem to the point that a house was built for her. When she finally put to bed, the child that was delivered to her had a full set of adult teeth (which was considered as a supernatural power), and his tears were blood. The woman declared that her young child would be the leader of the people, and upon her proclamation, there was a heavy downpour of rain, and that was how the child got his name (Deng), which means rain. Legend has it that Deng exercised authority over the people for years, and when he became old, he vanished in a storm.

17. Djakomba

Djakomba, also Djabi or Djakoba, is the supreme god and creator – the god of the sky with a voice of thunder and could strike people down with lightning – of the Bachwa people of the Democratic Republic of Congo. He is believed to be the creator of everything that exists, including the primordial human being (the Bachwa people) ergo the Bachwa people refer to themselves as the 'children of Djakomba.' The sky god provided humans with life and food for their sustenance; he was also responsible for the appearance of illness and death. Although the Bachwa believe that after people died, they were sent to the heavens to live with Djakomba, and they would not have to go through any adversity.

18. Dzivaguru

Among the Shona people of Zimbabwe, Dzivaguru is the god of water who also possessed ruling over the seasons and was apt to calling for the downpour of rain when he believed it to be necessary. The Shona people rely on the benevolence of the rain god, especially because a reliable source of rain is what ensures survival; therefore, they believed the rain deity to be quite generous and benevolent. They also believed that he was roaming around the land, using magic to perform various acts of kindness.

19. En-Kai

En-Kai means sky to the Massai people of Kenya. He is the supreme god and creator who brought forth rain and was also the deity of fecundity. He was a god of the sky and of the sun, while his wife Olapa was the goddess of the moon. The Massai people called him various names such as Parsai, meaning 'the one who is worshipped' and Emayian, which means 'the one who blesses.' The primeval man was created by the sky and sun deity and was called Naiteru-Kop; he and his wife were sent to the earth with livestock (sheep, cattle, and goats) to keep the earth and the natural resources within it for the sake of generations to come and thus, Naiteru-Kop and his family became the Massai ancestors.

A different tale holds that people came forth from a termite hole and decided to settle within the locality of the hole. A particular myth tells of the presentation of cattle to the Massai people; En-Kai told the primeval humans to leave their animal pens called *kraals* open at night, and while some obeyed, others did not. At night, noises from animals woke the people up, and when they looked outside, they saw cattle, goats, and sheep coming out of the termite hole and running into the *kraals* that were open. The Massai are the descendants of the people who left their *kraals* open, and those who did not are the present-day Kamba.

Another myth says that En-Kai asked Dorobo to go see him one morning. However, a Massai eavesdropped on the conversation and went to see En-Kai first. En-Kai believed the person to be Dorobo, and so he told the Massai to do a few things; after doing En-Kai's bidding, the Massai was to return to En-Kai in 3 days. Then, En-Kai eventually instructed the man to return to his hut and remain there no matter what; after that, En-Kai let down a rope made of pelt upon which cattle were sent to the earth. The Massai heard the noise and came out despite the warning. This broke the rope so that no more cattle were able to come down. Nevertheless, the Massai was contented with the ones he had gotten, explaining why the Massai had cattle while the Dorobo was forced to go hunting for wild game.

20. Eshu

Eshu or Esu is the god of chance, accident, and unpredictability of the Yoruba people of Nigeria. Amongst all the gods of the Yoruba people known as Orisa, he is one of the most important and complex. He had mastery of every language, and so he was the messenger of the supreme god, Olorun, who lived in the sky. Eshu was the mediator between humans and Olorun; he carried the messages and sacrifices of humans to Olorun. He also informed Olorun of the activities of both humans and the other gods, and whenever Olorun commanded it, Eshu delivered either penalties or rewards; furthermore, he gave an account of how worship and sacrifices were made. At the start of every rite, an offering had to be presented to Eshu, or else the ritual would fail. Eshu is believed to wait at gates and crossways, where he introduces chances and accidents into the lives of humans. Various myths tell of his intermediary role between forces that were in opposition, negotiating between the pantheon and re-establishing a balance in their relationship. The Yoruba's believe that divination – forecasting the future or fortune-telling – was handed down to them by Eshu. An aspect of Eshu portrays his benevolence and his protection, while another aspect of him shows him to be evil and his capability of leading humans to carry out evil activities.

One tale that exemplifies how much he enjoys stirring mischief shows how he caused a fight between two friends who both owned farms that bordered each other. Every single day, Eshu walked along the path, which separated both farms with a black cap on. Then a day came where he wanted to trick both men. He made a cap that had four colors (black, white, green, and red), which, contingent upon the angle it was seen, still appeared as one color. He put on his cap, with his pipe clung to his neck and staff to his back rather than his chest, he continued with his daily walk. The first farmer told his friend that he found it odd that Eshu was walking opposite the direction which he usually took when he walked in that path wearing a white cap rather than his usual black; his friend, on the other hand, answered saying that Eshu took his usual route while walking the path and that he was wearing a red cap. A fierce argument then broke out between the two, so they both went to visit their king to resolve the issue. While at the king's place, Eshu appeared and revealed that his cap had four colors and that if anyone was watching his pipe and staff instead of his feet, they would assume his motion was the opposite of what it actually was. Although he was naturally apt to causing dissension and strife, he always made a clean breast of his mischief in the end.

Eshu's mischief was not restricted to humans alone. He played tricks on the gods as well. A myth tells of how Obatala, who created land and humans, visited the god of thunder and lightning, Shango (Sango). Although Orunmila, who is the god of divination, had warned Obatala to not embark on the journey, Obatala insisted, and so Orunmila told him never to show any retaliation irrespective of what he faced. Obatala encountered Eshu on his way, who asked for Obatala's aid to place a bowl of palm oil upon his (Eshu's) head, while Obatala was helping to lift the bowl, oil spilled on his white garment. This forced him to go back home, change his garment and resume his journey; again, he encountered Eshu, who asked for his help to lift a bowl of oil, and when he did, the previous outcome was repeated. When the same thing happened the third time, Obatala did not change his garment but went on his journey; on his way, he saw one of Shango's horses which Eshu made to appear, running loose. Obatala caught the horse with the intention of returning it to Shango, but Shango's servants saw him first, and because of his dirty garments, they did not recognize him and taking him for a horse thief, they locked him in prison.

Many months and years went by while Obatala was in prison, and all through that time, he never protested. Soon, disaster fell upon the kingdom of Shango; rain never fell, and crops died. Upon consulting an oracle, Shango was told that someone was unjustly lying in his prison, and that was why the kingdom was suffering, and until that personality was released, the disasters would continue. Shango then visited his prison, and when he saw Obatala, he recognized him immediately and released him. Shango fell at the feet of Obatala and pleaded for pardon. Obatala granted his request, and rain once again fell in Shango's kingdom.

21. Gulu

Gulu is the sky god among the gods of the Baganda people of Uganda known as Lubaale, although the name was also used to refer to the heavens. Gulu was the next in hierarchy after the supreme deity, Katonda. Gulu fathered the god of death known as Walumbe, as well as Nambi that eventually married Kintu, the first king of Uganda.

22. Gurzil

Gurzil is the sun deity as well as the deity of prophecy to the Huwwara people of Libya. A two-horned Carthaginian (Carthage used to be an ancient city-state in the now Republic of Tunisia) god known as Baal Hammon is used to identify him and is represented with a bull. This deity was viewed as a guardian who, because of his precognition, served as a guide for humanity. The aspect that reflects him as a sun god was what made him able to drive out the darkness and bring light into the world.

23. Imana

Imana is the supreme god and creator of everything that exists as well as the omnipotent ruler of every living thing to the Banyarwanda, Hutu, and Tutsi people of Burundi and Rwanda. At the beginning of time, every living thing lived with him in the sky; death was not a lasting situation because Imana brought anyone who had died back to life within three days. One myth tells of a woman who had no child and begged the god for children; her wish was granted, and she bore three children with the condition that no one was to know where her children came from. Out of jealousy, the sister of the woman who had no children as well asked the woman to reveal how she got children and although she refused to tell for a while, she later revealed the secret to her sister. Imana's anger was kindled upon the woman because of her disobedience; the woman then killed her children so that she could quell his anger. The heavens opened and down fell the children to the earth, which was full of agony and asperity, and life was miserable for the children. After the woman and sister had asked the deity for pardon, he said he was going to bring them back to the sky when he felt they had gone through enough agony.

A story of how death came into existence suggests that death was personified as an animal that was hunted by Imana, who commanded humans to remain inside their houses while he hunted the animal so that death wouldn't have anywhere to hide. A certain woman visited her vegies garden, and death asked for her help, and she hid him underneath her skirt. Displeased by her disobedience, Imana declared that death would forever remain with humans.

Another tale says that death hid underneath the skirt of the woman, but she didn't know. Death went into the woman's house, and the woman passed away; the woman's death pleased her daughter-in-law. However, three days later, they saw that the grave of the woman was opened because Imana had brought the woman back to life, and she tried to resurrect. The daughter-in-law covered the soil to keep the woman in the grave; this happened day-after-day for three days, after which the grave grew silent. That the grave did not try to open again gave the daughter-in-law joy, but it also signified the permanence of death for humanity.

Another tale goes thus: A man was told that he would gain a long life from Imana if he was able to stay awake that night, but the man was unable to stay up. A snake eavesdropped on the conversation that Imana had with the man and went to wait on Imana; by mistaking the snake for the man, Imana said that when it grows old, it will be able to shed its skin and be born again. This is the reason why humans can die permanently while snakes are believed to have a long-lasting life.

24. Jok

Jok, also Jok Odudu, is the name given to the supreme deity and creator of the Acholi, Lango people of Uganda, the Alur people of the Democratic Republic of Congo and Uganda, and the Dinka people of Sudan. He was believed to possess ubiquity (he could be perceived in everything and every place). The celestial bodies are a part of his creation, so is the earth and everything that exists in it, including animals and humans to whom he taught agriculture and gave fire. He was also the god of fertility, and therefore, he made the ability to give birth possible. He sent down rain when humanity needed to grow their crops and ceased the rain so that humans could go hunting. His involvement in human matters was not direct as spirits who were also called *jok* were the ones who took part in the day-to-day activities of humans and accomplished the tasks that Jok wanted to be done. Lango culture believes that Jok was merged with the spirits, and so he was, in actuality, a combination of spirits in one deity.

A myth of how death came into existence tells that Jok intended to give humanity a fruit from the Tree of Life in order to make them immortal; when he invited them to the heavens to receive the fruit, they took time to respond, and this angered the supreme god, so he gave the fruit to the sun, the moon, and the stars. When the humans finally got to the heavens, Jok had no fruit left to give to them, and that is what explains why the celestial bodies are immortal, and the humans are not.

25. Juok

Juok, also Jwok is the supreme god and creator of the Anuak, Shilluk people of Sudan who are believed to have both male and female characteristics at the same time but usually referred to using 'he.' He birthed a lot of children such as an elephant, a buffalo, a lion, a crocodile, a dog and then the first humans, a boy and a girl. Juok became displeased with humanity, and he asked a dog to eliminate them; the dog, however, raised the children instead till they became adults. At the time, the earth became full of creatures, and the supreme god decided to group the creatures, assign them to a particular area of land together to provide them with weapons. Humans were the last he considered, and seeing this, the dog cognized that by the time Juok would be done, there would be no land or weapons left for humans, so he told the man to go tell the supreme god that he (man) was the elephant, lion, and buffalo; hearing this, Juok gave the man all the spears. At the arrival of the animals, there were no weapons left, so Juok gave the tusks to the elephant, claws to the lion, teeth to the crocodile, and horns to the buffalo. Using his spears, the man chased the animals and took for himself the best land.

A tale of how death came to be said that at the beginning of time, death was not a lasting situation. People usually died and returned back to life after three days. Juok, one day, decided that death should be the final end for one's life, and so he threw a rock into the river. The dog asked humanity to get the rock out, but no one paid him any attention. The dog couldn't get the rock out himself; however, he was able to break a huge part of it and took it home. Since then, humans started dying permanently, although because a huge part of the rock was broken, they could live long before they died.

26. Kalumba

Kalumba is to the Luba people of the Democratic Republic of the Congo, the supreme god, and creator who, at the beginning of time, sent a man and woman on an exploration of the universe. The man and woman found the place to be dark save for the presence of the moon, and they returned to him with the information, after which Kalumba made the sun to serve as a light for humans. He again sent the man and woman back to the earth with a dog, birds, spark rocks, iron, and the ability to reproduction, thus making them humanity's earliest parents.

Another tale says that humans lived with Kalumba in the beginning, but they had started fighting, so the god sent them to the earth where they first felt hunger, cold, illness, and death. Having being told by a diviner to return to the heavens to escape their predicament, humans built a high tower that reached the sky; on getting there, they beat drums to let the rest of humanity on earth know that they had gotten to their destination. Angered by the noise, the deity reduced the tower to rubble so no more humans could get to where he was.

A myth of the existence of death says that Kalumba was aware that both life and death would be on the same path to get to humanity, so he sent a goat and a dog to act as sentries on the path and let only life through in a bid to make humans immortals. An argument broke out between the dog and the goat regarding who would stand guard first. The goat pointed out that the dog would sleep off before yielding and allowing the dog to stand guard. It happened as the goat anticipated. Death slipped past because the dog slept off. When it was the goat's time to keep watch, it did not sleep, so it saw life when it tried to pass, although he did not know death had already gotten into the world.

27. Kanu

Kanu is the name given to the supreme god and creator of the Limba people of Sierra Leone. The different groups of the Limba have different names for the deity; the Safroko Limba called him Kanu, the Sela Limba called him Masala, and the Tonko Limba call him Masaranka. At the beginning of time, Kanu was living on earth, and then, creatures began attacking each other, and this displeased him, and even though the deity commanded that this be stopped, a python killed a deer and ate it. Then, ants ate the python, the fire destroyed the ants, and water quenched the fire; all of these occurrences made Kanu exile himself to the sky.

The story of how death came into being goes thus: Kanu had created a medicinal drug to make humans immortal, which he gave to a serpent to deliver it to humans, but a toad took the drug, and while it was hopping, all of the drug splattered. Kanu declined creating another drug, and then death came to Limba.

28. Katonda

Katonda is the name of the supreme deity of the Baganda people of Uganda. He was recognized as the father of the Baganda pantheon in the same manner as the first king, Kintu is recognized as the father of all living humans on earth. The Baganda thought of Katonda as a benevolent deity who preserved life and never brought harm or death to humans. He was the ultimate judge of humans, and the natural world was presided over by him via the spirits of deified heroes, incarnations of natural elements, and ancestors.

29. Khonvoum

Khonvoum is to the pygmy of Cameroon, Central African Republic, the Democratic Republic of the Congo, Gabon, and the Republic of the Congo; the supreme god and creator – most significant god among all the pygmy gods. He is also recognized as the god of the hunt and 'the great hunter'; his bow was made from two snakes, and it looked like the rainbow to humans. Humans were only able to contact this deity through an elephant named Gor – another myth says it's a chameleon. After he had created the universe, Kibuka let down to the earth, the primeval humans; legend has it that he created black people from black clay, white people from white clay, and used red clay to create pygmies. Pygmies live as hunters and gatherers in the bleak forests in Africa, and ten different populations exist, such as Aka, Ake, Baka, Benzele, Bongo, Efe, Gvelli, Mbuti, Tikar, and Tswa. Khovoum made provisions of animals and exuberant forest vegetation for them all; at night, the task of the god was to renew the sun so it could rise the following day. To do this, fragments of stars were collected by Khovoum, and he chucked them to the sun to revitalize it.

30. Kibuka

Kibuka is the god of war amongst all the gods of the Baganda people of Uganda. Humans conferred with the deity when they had to face an enemy and defend themselves. One myth of this people says that it was the deity's refusal to pay close attention to admonitions that resulted in his death. His brother, Mukasa sent him to the earth to aid Baganda people when they had to war against Nyoro, warning him not to let his enemies know his location and to never contact the women of Nyoro. On the first day of battle, Kibuka hid in a cloud and was firing arrows at the Nyoro people; the first day's battle was won by the Baganda, and they took Nyoro people, including women, as spoils. Kibuka had one woman sent to him, but she fled at night after discovering all his secrets and told the Nyoro people; the following day during the battle, archers of Nyoro launched a fusillade of arrows toward the cloud where Kibuka was hiding, which wounded him mortally.

31. Kiumbi

Kiumbi is the supreme god and creator of the Asu people in the Pare region of Tanzania. The supreme god is said to live in the sky like many of the gods in Africa. Kiumbi used to be close to the humans that he made, but because of their disobedience, he separated himself a great deal away from them, and the only means by which humans could commune with him was through the ancestors who acted as mediators between him (Kiumbi) and them (humans). The humans then sought to restore the proximity that existed between them and the deity, and to achieve this, they attempted to build a tower that reached the sky, but as they got closer to him, he went farther away. The more they tried to get close to him, it upset him so he sent a famine upon the earth, which killed every person on the earth save a boy and a girl from whom the new human race stemmed.

32. Kwoth

Kwoth is the supreme god and creator of the Nuer people of Sudan. Kwoth didn't particularly have any form to him, nor did he have a particular place where he stayed. Being Kwoth Nhial, which means a 'spirit who is in the sky', he was usually affiliated with and believed to reveal himself via all the bodies in the sky, which include the sun, the moon, and stars, as well as natural occurrences. The people believed that he fell in the rain, blew in the wind, and that he was also within thunder and lightning. The rainbow was referred to as 'god's necklace.'

Like many other myths of African civilizations, the Nuer people also believe that heaven and earth used to be connected with a rope, and at the time, there was no death. Whenever a person became old, they could use the rope to climb up to heaven for the deity to make them young again and then have them return to earth. On a certain day, however, a hyena climbed up the rope to the sky, and the Kwoth asked the spirits in the sky to keep a close watch on the hyena and stop it from returning to the earth because that could cause problems. But, the hyena somehow broke away, and on its way down, it severed the rope, hence cutting the link with the sky and the earth, and people could not climb up to the heavens anymore and be returned to their young selves and death entered the world.

33. Legba

Among the gods of the Fon people, Legba is the seventh and last son of the Mawu-Lisa, the creator. When Mawu-Lisa had divided up the regions of the world among her first six children, there was nothing left to give to Legba, so the creator made him her messenger. His job was to visit the domains of the other gods and then return with information to Mawu-Lisa, and for that purpose, Legba had the gift of being able to speak various languages so that if anybody, whether human or deity who wanted to convey a message to the supreme god, they could easily give the message to him and he would deliver it. Furthermore, he was in possession of the key to the gate that separated the world of humanity from the domain of the deities, and when it came to deciding the destiny of humans, he had a major role to play.

Legba was known to be very intelligent and crafty. There was a time when Mawu-Lisa sent him to earth to check on the god of the earth, Sagbata, who informed Legba that Hevioso (Sogbo) was preventing rain. Legba assured the earth god that he would inform Mawu-Lisa and then send a bird called Wutulu with instructions on how to proceed. Wutulu then came to Sagbata, telling him to build a great fire with smoke that would reach the heavens, and when Sagbata started the fire, Legba went to Mawu-Lisa with the message that the earth was on fire, so Mawu-Lisa ordered Hevioso to release rain on the earth. Legba was originally the reason why it stopped raining on the earth when he told Mawu-Lisa that there wasn't enough water in the heavens, and that was what led to the ceasing of a downpour.

34. Pishiboro

This is the supreme god of the Igwike people of Botswana, Namibia. At the beginning of time, the only thing in existence was just emptiness save for the supreme god Pishiboro. It was his death that brought about the creation of the universe. Legend has it that a puff adder bit the supreme god, and that was what killed him; the rocks and hills were created from the blood that poured out of his injures, and valleys were carved from his flailing body. Rivers and streams were created from the water that poured out of his body, and his hair formed the clouds from which the rain which gave life poured down.

After his resurrection, Pishiboro then created humans, and being unhappy with how they looked without hair, he gave them hair; but that only made them look like other animal creatures, so he made them again with hair only on certain parts of their bodies. After that, the supreme god shaped all the animals he had created into various forms, gave them names and functions. He then declared that all animals having horns were to be consumed as food; humans were not to be consumed. If they died of natural causes or were killed, they should be buried.

Goddesses

1. Abuk

Abuk is a goddess of the Dinka people of Sudan. This is the primeval woman whose status was raised up to the divine level so that she became the patron goddess of women and gardens. Abuk was in charge of handling any and all issues that concerned women, which included, for the most part, the growing of millet. A small snake is an allegory that is used to represent her. It is said that at the beginning of time, there was a rope linking the heavens, which were home to the supreme god, Nhialic, to the earth. The supreme god gave his permission for Abuk and her husband Garang (primeval man) to plant and grind a single millet a day to be consumed as food; however, a certain day came where Abuk became so hungry, in fact, that she planted a lot of millet cereals. She was made use of a hoe for her cultivation, and in the process, she struck Nhialic with her hoe by accident because the earth and the heavens were in close proximity; furious about this, Nhialic then severed the rope that linked the heavens to the earth and decided to longer meddle in human affairs.

As a result of this outcome, humans are forced to toil intensely in order for them to have food; furthermore, things like sicknesses and death found its way into the world. Some traditions believe that Abuk was the mother of a rain and fertility god by the name of Deng, who also is the one who mediates between humans and the supreme god.

2. Ala

Ala is also called Ale or Ali among the Igbo people in Nigeria. It is the name given to the earth goddess, who is also the goddess of fertility and daughter of the supreme god – Chukwu. Despite the fact that humans were created by Chukwu, he was distant from them; this is what differentiates between him and Ala because, unlike Chukwu, she was close to humans that she came to be recognized as the mother of the Igbo people. It is said that everything was brought forth from her – the earth was borne from her womb – and she took over the protection of the inhabitants of the earth. Since being the goddess of fertility, she made the female of the human species able to give birth, give life to children, and kept watch over them through their lifetime. She accepted people who died into her body (earth) and ruled over the ancestors because the rulership of the underworld belonged to her. The Igbo people believe that when a person dies, they become the earth and become one with Ala.

3. Ama

Ama or Ma is the name given to the creator – who may be a combination of two gods – among the Jukun people of Nigeria. At times, Ama has two aspects: a god (male) and a goddess (female). The female aspect of Ama is the Earth goddess believed to be the mother of the universe and counterpart of Chido, the sky god. Chido was the god that resided in the sky while Ama resided on the earth. Ama was the creator of the heavens, the earth, and everything that exists; since being the earth personified, she ruled the underworld known as Kindo, of which the Jukun people believe that every living thing originated from and where they will return to when they die. Ama is equated as a potter; it is said that she created the body of humans by building it up bone after bone, just as a potter makes a pot by building up clay. When Ama was done creating any human, Chido would descend from the sky and breathed life into the person so that they could come alive. When Ama created crops to give humans nourishment, Chido sent rain to help grow the crops.

4. Asaase Yaa

Asaase Yaa, also known as Aberewa or Asase Ya, is a goddess of the barren places of the earth among the Ashanti people of Ghana. She is the daughter of Nyame, the supreme god and creator, and some versions of her story say she is the mother of Asansi, the spider, a trickster, and a culture hero. Asaase Yaa or Aberewa had a long, sharp sword that was self-controlled to fight as long as she gave the order, and whenever she did, the sword killed everyone it ran into unless she ordered the sword to stop.

A tale of Anansi and Aberewa's sword goes thus: famine existed in the land, and the only storehouse that had food belonged to Nyame, so Anansi offered to become Nyame's agent and sell the food in his storehouse in exchange for Anansi's head to be shaved on a daily basis. Anansi always felt pain when his head was shaved, and people mocked his looks; so, he stole some of Nyame's food and ran to Asaase Yaa's house. He then asked her to protect him, and she agreed. A day came when the goddess left the house, and Anansi stole her sword and went back to Nyame, offering to protect him using the sword, should Nyame ever need protecting and Nyame gave his consent. When faced with enemies, Anansi commanded the sword to fight, and the army of the enemy was vanquished, but then Anansi forgot the words he had to utter to make the sword stop, and since the sword could not be stopped, it also destroyed Nyame's forces and killed Anansi as well. The sword then bound itself to the ground and turned into a plant that had sharp leaves, which can cut anyone that touches them. Since no one ever ordered the sword to stop, the plant still cuts people to date.

Chapter 5

Legends with animals as protagonists

Anansi

The tales of Anansi is one that is found throughout West Africa, with the ones originating from Ghana being among the best of tales. Anansi was an Akan folktale character, which means spider because it often assumed the shape of a spider. Anansi was considered to be a god of all knowledge of stories. He was a trickster who was well known for his creative and cunning nature. His ability to triumph and outsmart over more powerful opponents often portrayed him as a protagonist.

From Ghana, Anansi spread to Suriname, West Indies, Sierra Leone, where they were introduced by Jamaican Maroons, the Netherlands Antilles, Aruba, and Curacao.

Over time, Anansi had been represented with different names in many different ways like "Kwaku Ananse", "Ananse", "Anancy". Now, it is depicted as "Ba Anansi", "Kompa Nanzi", "Nancy, Aunt Nancy or Sis Nancy". Though often depicted as an animal, Anansi's representation also includes acting and appearing as a man. This gives a clue that Anansi was an anthropomorphized spider with the face of a man or a man with spider-like features.

In other folktales, Anansi had a family which included his long-suffering wife, Okonore Yaa. Other regions knew her as

Aso, Shi Maria, or Crooky. His firstborn son's name was Ntikuma. Tikelenkelen was his big-headed son. Afudohwedohwe was his pot-bellied son, while his son with spindly neck and legs was known as Nankonhwea. Also, not leaving out his beautiful daughter Anansewa whom Anansi in Efua's tale embarked on a mission to ensure she got the right suitor.

Anansi is synonymous with skill and wisdom in speech because his stories were exclusively part of an oral tradition. Anansi stories came to the limelight and was a major part of the Ashanti oral culture, which was seen in their kinds of fables, as was proven by R.S. Rattray's work recorded in both Twi language and English. Even Peggy Appiah attested that: "So well-known is he that he has given name to the rich tradition of tales on which so many Ghanaian children are brought up anansesem or spider tales."

The rest of the world came about the tales of Anansi through oral tradition. Most especially are the Caribbean people who were made aware of these tales by those who were enslaved during the Atlantic slave trade. Rather than the importance of Anansi to diminish socially, it became celebrated as a symbol of slave survival and resistance. The reasons being that Anansi was able to use his cunningness and trickery to turn the tables of oppression. This was a system used by slaves at that time to gain the upper hand from their taskmasters in the plantation environment.

The inspiring strategy of resistance, Anansi's tales were able to play multifunctional roles in the lives of slaves, thereby enabling enslaved Africans to establish a sense of continuity with their African past and offering them hope to transform and assert their identity within the boundaries of captivity. As was argued in historian Lawrence W. Levine's Black Culture and Consciousness, Africans enslaved in the new world majorly devoted "the structure and message of their tales to the compulsions and needs of their present situation."

Since Jamaica had the largest concentration of enslaved Ashanti, the version of Anansi's stories well preserved are those of the Jamaicans, and relating to their Ashanti origins, each story carries their own proverbs at the end. There is a proverb at the end of the story "Anansi and Brah Dead" that suggests that Anansi in times of slavery was referred to by his original Akan name: "Kwaku Anansi" or "Kwaku" being used interchangeably with Anansi. The proverb is: "If yuh cyan ketch Kwaku, yuh ketch him shut". This points to the time when the personification of death Brah Dead (the brother death or dry-bones) was chasing Anansi to kill him.

The proverb meaning: The target of revenge and destruction, even killing, will be anyone close to the intended, such as family members and loved ones.

In the diaspora, based on his penchant for ingenuity, Anansi's presence has been reinvented through an exchange that is multi-ethnic and beyond its Akan-Ashanti origin, seen in the diversity of names attributed to Anansi in his stories. From "Kuenta Di Nazi" to "Anansi-tori". Or is the 'Ti Bouki" character, the buffoon who was harassed constantly by "Ti Malice" or is it the Haitian trickster "Uncle Mischief" associated with Anansi references ti's exchange: "Bouki" is a word descending from the Wolof language referencing the hyena indigenous to them. Anansi roles beyond the era of slavery entertain just as they instruct, showing alongside his flaws, cleverness, and features the subversive just as the mundane. Anansi has now become both an idea that inspires and a cautionary tale against selfish desires that can lead to one's undoing. He is now evolved and considered a classical hero as compared to being seen as a trickster.

Popular Anansi stories

There exist many stories collected in the literature that have Anansi written all over it. Among which are;

Akan-Ashanti stories

How the sky-God stories became Anansi

This is Rattray version of the most commonly retold folktales as recorded in his book The Akan-Ashanti fork tales. In these tales, there were no stories in the world because the sky God Nyame, also known as Nyankonpon, had all the stories. Anansi wanted Nyame's stories, so he then went ahead to see the sky god so as to offer him money for his stories. Nyame was not convinced at Anansi proposition because other great kingdoms like Bekwai, Kokofu, and Asumengya had tried to do the same as well but could not pull it off. So, he was wondering how Anansi would succeed when others had failed. Anansi was not intimidated, rather he promised to do whatever it cost, and so, he went ahead to ask the sky god to name his price. Nyame played along since Anansi was so insistent.

Nyame's high price was the impossible labor he set, knowing that Anansi wouldn't be able to get the task done. The task was that Anansi had to capture four of the most dangerous creatures in the world, namely Osebo the Leotard, the fairy Mmoatia, the Mmaboron Hornets, and Onini, the python. Anansi promised to get the four dangerous creatures and even throw in his mother Ya Nsia as a bonus. Nyame encouraged him to be on his way, having accepted Anansi offer while Anansi, on the other hand, went about putting his schemes to motion.

First, Anansi went to his family and then told them about his plans, not excluding his mother also. He then sought the counsel of his wife Aso as to how to go about capturing Onini, the python. Aso told him to cut a branch from a palm tree along with strings creeper vine. Then he should head to the river where Onini stays, pretending to have been in a heated argument with her as touching the size and height of Onini's body that it was longer than the branch of a palm-tree. All this attempt was set at getting Onini's attention, thereby enabling his capture.

So, Anansi set out just as his wife had counseled him. On his way to Onini's place, he began to argue imaginatively that his wife claimed that Onini's body was longer than a full-grown palm tree branch. Onini overheard Anansi's argument and came out to find out what was going on. Having explained all to Onini, he decided to assist Anansi in proving that he was longer than the branch of a palm tree. This, he agreed to do unaware of Anansi's scheme. When he inquired what he should do, Anansi told him to go stretch against the branch of the palm-tree he had already cut down.

On stretching against the branch of the palm-tree, Anansi took the string creeper vine to tie Onini completely. Having done that, Anansi wasted no time in going over to Nyame's. It was on his way to Nyame's that he told Onini of the deal he has made. Nyame was quite impressed with Anansi's victory but also reminded him of the remaining three challenges, secretly rooting that Anansi would meet with failure soon.

Anansi went home to his wife to let her know of the successful capture of Onini. Now, he needed her counsel once again to capture Mmoboro Hornets, of which she gladly obliged him. She told Anansi to fill a gourd with water and take it to the Hornets, which Anansi did. Heading into the bush, he came across a swarm of hornets. Having crept to where the hornets were, he sprinkled some of the water on the gourd at the Mmoboro Hornets while he immersed himself in the remaining water.

Anansi then cut a banana leaf to cover his head. Out of anger, the Hornets flew to where Anansi was hiding. Anansi, removing the banana leaf from his head, told the Hornets that it had been raining, showing them the wet banana leaf as proof. He then told the Hornets that the only way they can avoid the danger called rain was for them to get into the gourd. This idea sounded nice to the Hornets.

Unaware of Anansi's intention, they all flew into the gourd. Quickly, Anansi covered the mouth of the gourd and set out to see the Sky God. Anansi then told the Hornets of his plan to trade them for the Sky God's stories, for at this time, it was already too late for the Hornets. The Sky God accepted the Hornets from Anansi, congratulated him for his success thus far then reminded him that the task is far from completion. Anansi, leaving the Sky God's place, headed home.

On getting home, Anansi told his companion of his success. Now Osebo the Leopard was his next target. As usual, his wife counseled him. This time around, she told him to dig a hole and then cover it to catch the Leopard. Having understood the plan, he left home to where Osebo the Leopard was always found. Anansi dug a big hole around the place and then covered it with brushwood, knowing that there was no way the Leopard would miss stumbling into the hole. Coming back the next morning, just as he has predicted, he found the Leopard in the pit. Feigning ignorance and sympathetic at the same time asked the Leopard if he was drunk since he had once cautioned the Leopard about his drinking. Anansi then offered to help the Leopard but claimed that he was afraid for his life, saying that if he helped the Leopard out of the pit, the Leopard was going to eat him. The Leopard promised not to harm him, and so Anansi reached for his knife, cut down two long sticks, and began to let it down into the hole. As the Leopard was attempting to scale the sticks and escape, Anansi threw his knife at the Leopard, and the haft of his knife hit the Leopard on the head, rendering him unconscious.

Anansi then went in to capture the Leopard. Just like the other victims of Anansi's schemes, he never failed to tell them his deal with the Sky God and how he desired to get the Sky God's stories. Nyame, receiving the Leopard from Anansi, still was not convinced that Anansi could accomplish all his tasks.

Anansi returning home, decided another time to capture Mmoatia the Fairy. Thinking through on how to capture the Fairy, Anansi came up with the idea of carving an Akua doll. Then Anansi got some sap from a gum tree and rubbed it on the doll till it became very sticky. Anansi was not so satisfied with what he had done, so he pounded some mashed yams (eto) and cover the doll's hand with it.

He then filled a basin with some mashed yams and tied some of his silk around the doll's waist so as to manipulate it. Having been satisfied with his creation, he headed straight to the land of fairies and placed the Akua doll in front of the Odum tree, majorly where fairies congregated with the basin and eto in front as bait.

This he did while he waited for the fairies behind the Odum tree. Soon, some fairies came along, with one lured away from her sister. On getting to where the Akua doll was, the fairy implored the doll if she could have some of her eto, Anansi then tugs the string around the doll's waist, causing it to nod her head in response. The fairy then quickly went to her sister and asked for permission to eat some eto, which they agreed.

The Mmoatia went back to the Akua doll and ate to her fill, and after which, she thanked the Akua doll, but this time did not get a response because Anansi refused to tug the string. The Mmoatia was not pleased by the attitude of Akua doll, so she called out to her sisters, who advised her to slap the doll. On doing that, her hand got stuck.

The Mmoatia beckoned on her sisters, who then encouraged her to use her other hand, and again, the second hand got stuck on the face of the Akua doll. Once more, the Mmoatia called out to her sisters, and this time they advised her to bludgeon the doll with the rest of her body and that she would be successful. This, she also did and was completely married to the Akua doll. Anansi came out from his hiding place and used the remaining string to tie the fairy to the doll.

Quickly, Anansi went back home to his mother and reminded her of his agreement with the Sky God for his stories, and she was part of the deal. His mother complied and went alongside him and Mmoatia to go see Nyame. Anansi presented both his mother and the Mmoatia to Nyame, who was now really amazed at the spider's success. Nyame then summoned the elders of his kingdom, the Akwam chiefs, the Kontire, the Adontem general of his army, the Oyoko, Ankobea, Kyidom, and lastly, the Gyase.

The Sky God then told everyone present of the task he gave to Anansi and presented the evidence, including Anansi's mother Ya Nsia before everyone and how Anansi was able to accomplish all when other great kingdoms had failed. He then relinquished the rights to his stories, that they would no longer be called by his name anymore.

From then onward, the Sky-God's stories became Anansi's stories and would be known as the spider stories for eternity. The people rejoiced alongside Nyame that day at Anansi's victory, and that is why every story, no matter the theme, is called a Spider story.

Take note that they exist substantial variants of this tale, like Haley's omitting Aso and Ya Nsia while retelling it. The Tiger became the one from whom the stories came from, according to a Caribbean version. Another common version presented Mmoatia as a solitary fairy that can turn invisible. Another version that exists does not require Anansi to capture a python.

Lightning Bird

The Impundulu, which is translated as "lightning bird" or Thekwane (or Izulu) is a folklore creature of the tribes of South Africa, which includes the Zulu, the Xhosa, and the Pondo. The Impundulu assumed the form of a black and white bird, having the size of a person capable of summoning lightning and thunder with its wings and talons. The bird is a vampiric in nature affiliated with witchcraft. The impundulu, being the servant of a witch doctor, attacks the witch's enemies. Its taste for blood is insatiable and does take the form of a handsome man to seduce women.

The hammer-kop, among certain African tribes, is believed to be the true lightning bird. While others believed that the true lightning bird only manifests itself through lightning, only in rare cases does it show up as a bird, and that is when it wants to reveal itself to women. With this many forms, the bird's true nature is imaginary; Like the village girl that described the bird that ran up to her hole and left claw marks on her body before flying into the clouds to be a black rooster-like bird. At another place, the lightning bird was described as having feathers like those of a peacock or a fiery red tail, bill, and legs.

The lightning bird has been described as a winged creature with the size of a man by most persons who have sighted the bird in one or another. Other than it being a huge black and white bird of prey, it is also said that the bird does mask itself as a man when need be.

Power

The fats of the bird can either be considered as a valuable component for traditional medicine or as the fuel needed by the bird when it wants to set things on fire by throwing down a lightning strike. One can come about this fat in two ways, either by catching the bird at the point when the lightning strikes the ground or by digging the bird up from an underground cavity at the spot. Furthermore, the bird is believed to lay large eggs underground at the very spot of the lightning strike. Now this laying of eggs could serve as a good or bad omen when the ground is dug to procure the eggs or dispose of it. The bird is also compared to a vampire because it is immortal. Legend has it that not only does the bird outlives its masters, but it can also equally be passed from mother to daughter carrying out the bidding of its owner. This bird cannot be killed by stabbing or gunshots. It cannot be poisoned or even drowned. The only known weakness of the lightning bird is that it can be killed by fire.

Cultural Significant

The witch doctor, as it is seen in most tribes, is the only one that has the essential role of dealing with the lightning bird. Also, a supposed extract from the flesh of the bird can be used by the witch doctor to track thieves, mind control both law-abiding citizens and criminal masterminds in that society. The lightning bird is the witch confidant as it is most times seen on the back of witches that turned themselves into a hyena. The impundulu is considered the witch right-hand man as it is greatly feared. It can wreck-havoc, cause illness, and bring bad luck to a person when it is dispatched by a witch to do her bidding.

Other Vampire birds

The lightning bird has similarities with the vampire finch, which is confined to the Galapagos Islands. According to legend, the lightning bird is a vampire bird that feeds on blood. For instance, it feeds off other birds in animal form and, while in a human form, feeds off humans. The vampire finch, on the other hand, draws blood from sleeping sea birds by pecking them at the base of their feathers. There is another bird found in Africa called the red-billed Oxpecker.

This bird can be seen on cattle whenever there is fresh blood. Among these birds that have a taste for blood, none is as dangerous as the lightning bird.

A South African man in 2005 was convicted of culpable homicide after killing a two- year old whom he believed to be a lightning bird but in human form.

Chapter 6

Legends with heroes as protagonists

These are kings, queens, chiefs, and other leaders all across the continent of Africa who stood and fought, laying down their lives for what they believed. Among these heroes are:

King Sekhukhune 1881

In the year 1861, after the death of his father Sekwati I, Sekhukhune became the king of the Pedi or Bapedi nation, usurping Mampuru II, the supposed heir to the throne of the Pedi nation.

In 1881, he was arrested in the ZAR capital in Pretoria after he waged war against the Boer of the South African Republic, the British empire, and the Swazi. He met with defeat at the hand of the British and 10,000 Swazi warriors.

On August 29th, 1882, the London Times, usually not known for writing on African ruling Affairs, wrote a tribute to Sekhukhune after he was assassinated by Mampuru II in 1882. Mampuru, on the other hand, was later hanged in Pretoria by ZAR the year following.

Shango of the Oyo Empire

Shango was the king who brought prosperity to the Yoruba people of the Oyo empire. He was the third king of the Oyo empire and has so many stories and myths surrounding him. For many Afro-Caribbean religions, Shango stands as the cornerstone of them all.

According to the Yoruba religion, Shango (Changó or Xangô in Latin America), is one of the principal ancestors of the Yoruba people and the popular Orisha of thunder. He is considered a focal point in the Santeria religion of the Caribbean as he represents the Oyo people of West Africa. During the Atlantic slave trade, the Oyo empire sold people, a lot of whom were then taken to South America and the Caribbean. This is the main reason why any Orisha initiation ceremony performed anywhere across the New World within the past hundred years has always been done according to the ancient traditional ceremony performed in the Oyo empire. This is the most complete traditional ceremony that has arrived on the shores of America.

Shango's sacred number is 6, while the color "red and white" are his sacred colors. Oshe is his symbol, which is a representation of swift and balanced justice. In general, Shango is the owner of the art of dance, the beta (3 double-headed drums), and music.

Jaja of Opobo

Early Life

Jubo Jubogha as he was named by his first master, was born in Igbo land and was sold as a slave to Bonny trader at the age of twelve. Later on, he was sold to the powerful head of the Opobu Manila Group of Chief Alali. This enterprising and gifted individual called Jaja by the British eventually became one of the most powerful men in the eastern Niger Delta.

The Niger Delta was the site of unique settlements called city-states. It is where Niger empties itself into the Gulf of Guinea in a system of intricate waterways.

Like the other city-states, Bonny rose to prominence and gained its wealth from the profits of the slave trade right from the 15th to the 18th centuries. In Bonny, anyone who was successful in business could attain prestige and power. As for Jaja's case, a hard-working slave could work his way up to the head of state because the house was a socio-political entity and was the basic unit of the city-state.

After the abolition of the slave trade in 1807, the trade-in oil which dethroned the trade-in slave began to reign in the 19th century. This trade became so lively that the region was called the Oil River areas.

Since the producers in the hinterland were prohibited from trading directly with the Europeans on the coast, the Houses of Bonny and other city-states controlled the palm oil trade both internally and externally. The Europeans were afraid of malaria and, as such, their reason for never leaving the coast.

The Rise of King Jaja

Jaja quickly became the head of the Anna Pepple House, absorbing other houses and increasing its activities as well as its influence because he was shrewd in business and politics.

Soon, he increased operations in the hinterland and a growing number of European contacts. Because of a power tussle among rival factions in the houses at Bonny, the faction led by Jaja went its own way, thereby establishing a new settlement called Opobo. He declared his independence from Bonny and became King Jaja Opobo.

Opobo was strategically located between the production areas of the hinterland and Bonny, which King Jaja capitalized on in controlling trade and politics in the Niger Delta. This he did that at the end of his ascendancy, fourteen out of eighteen Bonny houses had relocated to Opobo.

Jaja became so wealthy and powerful in a few years that he was now shipping palm oil by himself directly to Liverpool. British consul was not pleased with this latest development, so Jaja was offered a treaty of protection that, in return, the chiefs surrendered their sovereignty. Jaja refused and was assured rather vaguely that nothing would happen to his authority nor sovereignty of Opobo.

The Scramble for Africa and the fall of Jaja

Jaja continued on the path of regulating trades and levy duties on British traders. He went as far as stopping trade on the river till one British firm paid the levy duties. Despite British threats to destroy Opobo through bombing, Jaja refused to yield to the order of the British Consul to put an end to these activities. The scramble for Africa had already taken place unknown to Jaja and Opobo was now part of British territories. In this era, gunboat diplomacy was the method of settling international issues, and Great Britain fancied using her Naval power to negotiate terms that were more favorable to her people.

Jaja was arrested and sent to Accra when he was lured aboard the British Consul's warship. He was back to St. Vincent (Saint Vincent and the Grenadines), West Indies, after he was tried and found guilty of blocking the highways of trade and breaking the trade treaty. He died en route, four years later when he was permitted to return to Nigeria from exile.

Jaja exposed the British imperialism through his effective resistance and persevering insistence on African independence. He became the first victim who had suffered in the hands of foreign territorial intrusion. The news of Jaja and what became of him in the hands of Britain quickly spread like wildfire throughout the whole Niger Delta that other Chiefs, out of fear, surrendered quickly.

The British trader wasted no time in boycotting the middleman and dealing directly with the palm oil producers as soon as Quinine was discovered as the cure of malaria. This led to the decline of the city-states.

The death of Jaja was a victory for Britain as it eventually led to the colonization of the Niger Delta region before the end of that century.

Queen Amina of Zaria

The heart of the Hausa realm comprises of the seven original Hausa lands. This includes Daura, Katsina, Kano, Zazzau, Gobir, Garun Gabas, and Rano, which covers an area of approximately 1,300 square kilometers. In the 16th century, the capital of Zazzau was built by the Queen Bakwa Turunku and named it after her youngest daughter. The state of Zazzau was later renamed Zaria, which in present-day Nigeria is a province and a traditional kingdom.

However, the Legendary Amina, the elder daughter of Queen Bakwa, was the one that inherited her mother's warlike nature. At age 16, Amina (or Aminatu) was given the traditional title of Magajiya when her mother was made a queen. Magajiya was a title that speaks of honor and respect meant for the daughters of the Monarch. Amina was known for her bravery and military exploits as she spent time developing her military skills. A song was even written in her honor to celebrate "Amina, the daughter of Nikatau as a woman capable of doing what a man can do."

The architectural design that created the strong earthen walls surrounding her city was credited to Amina. This is a prototype used for the fortification in all Hausa states. Later, many of these fortified walls, known as Ganuwar Amina or Amina's walls, were built around the territories she had conquered.

Every of her conquest was of two folds; the first was to extend her nation beyond its main borders, and the second one was to reduce each conquered city to a position of a vassal.

It was stated by Sultan Muhammad Bello of Sokoto that "She made war upon these countries and overcame them totally so that the people of Katsina paid tribute to her and the men of Kano". She also made war on cities of Bauchi till her kingdom reached the sea in the south and the west." Likewise, according to the chronicle of Kano, she led her armies as far as Nupe." "The Sarkin Nupe sent her (i.e., the princess) 40 eunuchs as well as 10,000 kola nuts. She was the first in the Hausa land to own eunuchs and kola nuts."

In as much as Amina was a notable gimbiya (Princess), there exist so many theories as to the time of her reign. Some theories even doubt if she was ever Queen, to begin with. While one theory is of the view that she reigned from approximately 1536 to 1573. Another says that she became a queen right after her brother, Karama's death in 1576. While yet another one claims that she was never a titular queen even though she was a de facto ruler and a princess.

One thing is certain, despite the inconsistencies in these theories and that's over a 34 years period, the border of Zaira was extended greatly through her many conquests and the incorporation of territories conquered. As a result of the extension of Zaira beyond its primary borders and its growth in prominence, it became the center of the North-South Sahara trade and East-West Sudan trade.

Queen Nzingha of Ndongo (1582–1663)

Nzinga of Ndongo and Matamba

The Portuguese stake in the slave trade was threatened in the 16th century by both France and England, and for that reason, the Portuguese relocated their trading activities southward towards Congo and South-West Africa. In the final phase of their conquest of Angola, the Portuguese met with stiff opposition from a head of state, a queen who was equally a military leader.

Professor Glasgow, of Bowie Maryland, outlined some important aspects of her life: "Her extraordinary story begins about 1582, the year of her birth. She was referred to as Nzingha, or Jinga, but was better known as Ann Nzingha. She was the sister of the then-reigning King of Ndongo, Ngoli Bbondi, whose country was later called Angola. Nzingha was from an ethnic group called the Jagas. The Jagas was an extremely militant group who formed a human shield against the Portuguese slave traders. Nzingha never accepted the Portuguese conquest of Angola and was always on the military offensive. As part of her strategy against the invaders, she formed an alliance with the Dutch, who she intended to use to defeat the Portuguese slave traders.

Nzinga became Queen of Ndongo in 1623 at the age of 41. She preferred to be called a king and, as such, forbade her people from calling her Queen. She loved dressing in a man's clothing when leading her armies to war.

Later on, in her life, in the year 1659, at the age of seventy-five, she signed a treaty with the Portuguese, which in any way brought her no Joy. Nzinga resisted and fought the Portuguese all through her adult life until her death in 1663. African bravery doesn't stand a chance against the Portuguese gunpowder. After her death, the Portuguese had access to expand their slave trade.

Usman Dan Fodio

Shaihu Usman Dan Fodio was a preacher, writer, Sultan of Sokoto, and an Islamic reformer. He was an hausa fulani living in present-day Northern Nigeria. He was known as an Islamic revivalist who lived in the city-state of Gobir. Usman did not encourage the education of women in the religious matter, but that several of his daughters are scholars and writers, with Princess Nana Asmau being the most prominent one.

In his own right, Dan Fodio is a revered religious thinker. He studied classical Islamic science, theology, and philosophy. Dan Fodio, using his influence, sought approval to create a religious model town in Dagel, which was his hometown. Following his teacher Jibri ibn 'Umar argument that it was the duty and power of religious movement to create the ideal society that is free from oppression and any form of vice.

Dan Fodio became the reigning Commander of the Fulani empire, which was then the largest state in Africa after the fulani Holy War. Already vast in Islamic law, he worked to establish an efficient system of government grounded in Islamic law as well. By the time of the war, Usman was already advanced in age, so he retired and handed command to his son Muhammad Bello who is the Sultan of Sokoto.

Uprising of Dan Fodio inspires these Western Jihadis to follow the same: those of Massina Empire founder Seku Amadu, Toucouleur Empire founder El Hadj Umar Tall (who married one of dan Fodio's granddaughters), Wassoulou Empire founder Samori, and Adamawa Emirate founder Modibo Adama, who served as one of dan Fodio's provincial chiefs.

Chapter 7

Creation myths and legends from Africa

How Things Came to Be

There exist many myths that explain how the world came into existence. The Dogon say that twin pairs of creator spirits or gods called Nummo hatched from a cosmic egg. Other groups also speak of the universe, beginning with an egg. People in both southern and northern Africa believed that the world was formed from the body of an enormous snake, sometimes said to span the sky as a rainbow.

The Fon people of Benin tell of Gu, the oldest son of the creator twins Mawu (moon) and Lisa (sun). In the form of an iron sword, Gu came to earth and then became a blacksmith. He was tasked with one thing, and that was to prepare the world for people. He taught humans how to make tools, which in turn enabled them to grow food and build shelters. The San Bushmen of the south say that creation was the work of a spirit named Dxui, who was alternately a man and many other things, such as a flower, a bird, or a lizard.

African Bushmen creation myths

People living on the earth today were not always like that. There was a time when animals and humans lived peacefully underneath the earth with the Kaang, who is considered the Great Master and Lord of all existence. Humans and animals coexisting underneath the earth understood each other. No one suffered any lack. There was light everywhere, even though there's no existence of a sun. It was during this time of perfect happiness that the Kaang began planning how he wanted life above the surface to look like.

Kaang went about the creation of wonders of the world above by first creating wondrous trees whose branches stretched across the entire country. So, he dug a huge hole at the base of the wondrous tree reaching all the way down to the world below the surface where humans and animals lived. He led the first man up when he was done furnishing the world above.

After the first man was taken topside, the first woman came along also through the hole. Then every other person followed suit in coming through the hole. Kaang began helping the animals through. Some of the animals even dug their way through the tree, racing to the top. Soon, the surface was filled with people and animals totally amazed at the new world.

Kaang then gathered everyone together and began to admonish them to live peacefully with one another. He instructed the men and women not to build a fire in this new world or risk evil befallen them. They all agreed in unison, so Kaang left them and went to a secret place where he could watch the world he had created.

The people and animals soon began to enjoy the sun and the feel it had on their skin. When it was night, and the sun disappeared, darkness fell upon the people, and they were greatly distressed. They were cold and couldn't see each other like the animals do in the dark. Someone among them suggested that they built a fire that will give them light and keep everyone warm. This they did, ignoring the warnings of Kaang. As soon as the fire was built, all the animals, out of fear and mistrust for the humans, ran to the mountains and cave.

The people's disobedience came at the cost of them losing their relationship with the animals because they could no longer understand the animals or communicate with them. The seat of trust had now become that of fear between the humans and the animals.

The Bushmen of Africa believes that rain, wind, and thunder have an element of life in them just as plant and animals do. They are of the belief that the human eyes only see the external or body form and that inside the body is a spirit that is alive. That this spirit can move from one person: from a woman to a leopard or from a man to a lion. This is equally the reason why animals exist in the Bushmen of Africa myths.

The Yoruba of Nigeria

All that existed from the beginning was water, land, and sky, and Olorun, who was the ruler of the sky and the creator of the sun, was in charge of things. So, Obatala, a firm believer that the world needed more and who was equally a god, went to Olorun to ask for permission to create lands for all living things to exist. After being granted permission by Olorun, Obatala paid Olorun's first son Orunmila who is also the God of Prophecy, a visit to inform him of his intentions of creating the earth. For his mission to be a success, Orunmila told him to obtain items like a gold chain that would enable him to reach to the water below, a snail's shell filled with sand, palm nuts, a hen, and a black cat, all of which he was to carry in a bag. Obatala set out on his mission first by hanging the gold chain in the sky, then using it as a ladder to climb down. He could only go as far as the length of the gold chain is. Obatala dumped the sand from the snail's shell on the earth with the hen he was carrying. The hen scratches on the sand spreading it around to form the first solid land on earth.

Letting go of the chain, Obatala landed on the earth and called the place of his landing "Ife". He planted the palm nut he came down with, which sprout up to be a palm tree. The cat kept him company while he began to create figures like himself with clay since he was lonely. While still creating, he decided he needed a drink and, as such, made wine out of the juice of the palm tree. While still working, he drank until he was drunk, and the image he created became deformed. Olorun breathed life into the deformed figures, and they turned into human beings. Realizing that his drunkenness had led to the deformity of his creature, he vowed to be the protector of those born deformed. The first Yoruba village at Ife was formed by the first human created by Obatala. Thereafter, Obatala returned to the sky, splitting his time between the sky and Ife.

Olokun, who is the ruler of the sea, was not pleased with Obatala because he never sought her approval before creating land. So, she sent flooding to Obatala's village, Ife, which destroyed half of Obatala's kingdom. The remaining survivors sent Eshu, the messenger of the gods to Obatala and Olorun, asking for help. In response to their plea, Orumila went to earth, causing the water to retreat.

Olokun still was not satisfied, so she challenged Olorun to a weaving contest knowing that he was not a good weaver. Olorun accepted the challenge and sent in a chameleon instead of who mimicked all of Olokun's fabric; Olokun accepted defeat when she saw that she could not win.

The above creation myth originated from the Yoruba people of Nigeria. Ancient Yoruba people were more likely to relate with their city-state than with the Yoruba people as a whole. This is equally the reason why the Yoruba people often quarreled with nearby city-states.

The Yoruba people considered Ife to be very sacred since it was their principal city. This creation myth tried to explain the origin of the Yoruba's sacred city Ife and the creation of humanity.

Bumba Creation

Bumba is the creator of the sky, the sun, and the moon. He created human beings when he was done creating the African cosmogony. The African Cosmogony beings created one another and are not more important than the human beings that came after them. Also, Bumba's three sons followed in their father's footsteps in the creation process. This story also welcomed the support of the Bushongo's nature of communalism. The need for unity for the community and also the earth at large is the major lesson learned from this myth.

The Zimbabweans

This creation myth saw Modimo as the creator of Zimbabwe. He is the custodian of everything good and also had great power to destroy things, bringing natural disasters and devastation in his wake. He was the element of water when he was good and lived in the East. He belonged to the element of fire when he was bad and lived in the west. Modimo is responsible for the sky, earth, light, root, and he is a rare breed. The first and only of his kind.

The Zulu of Southern Africa

The ancient one Unkulunkulu came from uthlanga or reed and with him came cattle and people. After he was created, he created the earth and all his creatures. The people knew how to make fire and fend for themselves because he taught them. A part of him lives in everything he had created, for he is the beginning of all creation.

The creation Myth of Lower Egypt

The sun god, Ra came out from Nun, a body of water that is so chaotic and was the only thing in existence. Independently, he gave birth to Shu, the god of air, and Tefnut, the goddess of water. Together, they produced the god of earth Geb and Nut, the goddess of the sky. The first humans that existed came out of Ra's tears but were destroyed because of their rebellion. Ra's resentment of the earth caused him to return to the heavens leaving his son Shu to rule the earth. Nut got married to Geb and gave birth to Osiris, Horus, Set, Isis, and Nepthys. Set was a representation of evil, while Osiris represented good. A story exists of Osiris and Set rivalry.

The Berbers of North Africa

A man and a woman unaware of their sex lived together before creation began. They came to the realization that they were different on the day where disagreement ensued between them at the drinking well. The woman's insistence that she must drink first was shoved aside by the man, and the bottom of her clothes was opened on falling to the ground. The now intrigued man inquired about her body, and she said that it represented something good. Eight nights, he stayed with her, and fifty sons and fifty daughters were the product of that eight nights. Surprised by their many children decided to send them above ground who expanded the earth and created mankind.

The Oromo of Ethiopia

By way of a barrier of the stars, the creator Waqa distanced himself from the earth by living in the sky. He is a firm believer in persuasion and trickery. Not so a believer in punishment. He asked his creation man to make a coffin for him, and when it was completed, he tricked and locked them inside the coffin, sending them to the flat earth. The landscape of the earth was formed when he brought a rainstorm that lasted seven years. He released the men from the coffin unharmed, forming women from his blood as soon as the earth was completed. Thirty children were produced to these men who were not pleased with the number of their children. And so, Waqa turned half of the children into animals.

The Akan of Ghana

Nana Nyame, who is the Sky-God, was the main creator. Abrewa lived on earth with her children. They had access to their god through the process of preparing food. Soon, their god was not pleased with this practice anymore, so he moved higher so that there would be a distance between him and Abrewa. Abrewa then asked her kids to build a tower using mortars. Originally, where one mortar was needed to reach their god, she instructed her children to replace the top mortar with one at the bottom resulting in the collapse of the tower and the suffering of her children.

Chapter 8

Influence of other cultures and religions

African culture has greatly been influenced by other cultures, and over the years, the beliefs, customs, and traditions of Africans have been entangled with cultures from other continents. While some people argue that this influence has made positive impacts than negative impacts, others are of the notion that the negative impact of other cultures and religions in the African culture outweighs the positive impact.

Although Africa has diverse cultures gotten from the 54 different countries that are in it, the cultural identity and heritage of most of these countries have been undermined and almost forgotten because of the enormous impact that other cultures and religions have made.

There are terminologies that have been used by different scholars to describe the influence of other cultures and religions on African culture; the ones that are mostly used are civilization and globalization.

Civilization is the imposition of one's standard of culture, beliefs, and traditions on other people, arguably with the intent of achieving a higher standard of behavior while globalization is the idea of interacting and integrating one's culture with other cultures in other to become intertwined.

The earliest form of civilization in Africa started with the influence of the Romans on the Egyptians, which later went further to the Nubia, the Maghreb, and the horn of Africa. Other European countries such as Germany, France, Portugal, and Britain also contributed to the influence made to the African culture. It was said that the French and the Portuguese were able to accept an African as either French or Portuguese if the individual is ready to give up all African culture and adapt their ways of which. After that, they were separated from the rest of the people and defined as the civilized ones.

The Arabs began to invade into North Africa from the middle east in the 7th century A.D, of which. The major influence they made was the Islamization of the North Africans, which later spread to other parts of Africa.

The influence of the South Asians settled in the regions of Kenya, Uganda, South Africa, and Tanzania, and the earliest form of contact that the south Asians had with the Africans goes back to at least 2000 years back; the general migration history of the Asians to Africa was documented from 19th century onward when the number of Asians in East Africa grew from 6,000 to 54,000. The South Asians include the Indians (Hindu), the Muslims, Jains, Sikhs, Goans, and others. This migration brought about economic changes and the influx of other religions, which also influenced the culture of the Africans.

As for the North Americans, their influence started during the 1800s when the western tourist, imperialist, and the explorers began to search out the heart of Africa for natural resources and gemstones, thereby bringing along with them the American culture and Christianity.

The aspects of African culture that has been influenced by other cultures include:

1. Politics

Before the migration of other countries to Africa and the civilization of the Africans; authority, and power of a community is usually bestowed on every member of that community, but as a result of ontology, the power is usually vested to a worthy leader or group of leaders of which their job is to exercise power on behalf of every member of the community and also serve as their representatives in the face of other communities. They are usually known as kings, chiefs, and such other names, depending on the community. These chosen leaders are always dedicated to the growth and well-being of the community, of which there was little or no corruption, coup, or any political riots among them, unlike today.

The influence of the other cultures, predominantly the western culture, led to the abandonment of the African political culture, of which the Democratic culture of politics, which is linked to the westerners, was adopted. This results in African politics being slowly emptied of its quintessence and becoming a game of scandal for various corrupt leaders. The contemporary African politicians no longer see themselves as a representative of the people with the sole mandate of serving them. The leaders today fight, kill, and commit all sorts of atrocities just to step into the position of power. This does not only show that Africans neglected their culture of politics and leadership, but it also shows that whatever political rule that becomes normalized and adopted by the westerners will eventually be normalized and accepted by the Africans, whether it is beneficial or not.

2. Religion

Religion constitutes a very important and intricate part of the African society, and because of this, most of the social, political, and economic activities of the Africans are usually seasoned with religious rites and rituals.

Due to the diversity of the continent, Africa has a lot of religions; although no single religious beliefs and practices can be directly identified as African, there were myths and ritual processes across the geographic and ethnic boundaries that were known to have originated from Africans.

Myths were peculiar to each religion, as discussed earlier in this book, and these serve as the basis of their religion and belief practices. These beliefs, practices, rituals, and religious rites were held in high regard and practiced by every member of each community, but the influence of other cultures has drastically modernized and changed most of these traditional beliefs and practices.

Most present-day Africans are unaware of the religious beliefs and traditional rites practiced by their forefathers. The influence of other cultures has brought in Christianity, and Islamic religion, which is the major and the most practiced religions in Africa today. Some people have ignorantly commented that these religions are part of the indigenous traditional religions in Africa because of the enormous impact that they have made in African society.

The influence of Christian cultures on the African traditional religion was achieved by the Christian missionaries who came from the west, and also, the returned African slaves that were converted to Christians also contributed to the widespread of Christianity in Africa. The Islamic culture began to spread when the Arabs crossed into North Africa from the middle east, of which the North Africans are said to have the highest population of Muslims in Africa.

3. Lifestyle

The influence of other cultures has immeasurably affected the lifestyle of Africans, starting from what they eat to dressing and entertainment. Most of the heritage and culture of the Africa that has to do with lifestyle has been abandoned, and other cultures of the immigrants and colonialist have been adopted. These influenced lifestyles include:

African Dishes: Historically, African countries, like all other countries, are known for some food general to them, and they have also adopted foods from those who migrated from other continents. These traditional African dishes are passed from one generation to the next. It serves as a means of preserving cultural identity, and not only are the traditional dishes being passed down generationally, the adopted dishes that were introduced to the Africans by the immigrant were also being eaten, sold, and the recipes were also transferred to the children.

Some Africans prefer eating dishes belonging to other countries more than their indigenous meals, which show the considerable influence that other cultures have made on the dishes eaten by the Africans. As the world becomes globalized, dishes of different cultures can be assessed by anyone across the globe.

African Clothing: African clothing is the traditional garment worn by the people of Africa. Since Africa is a very big and diverse continent, traditional garment differs throughout each community, some communities are known for wearing dresses with bright colors, some cultures wear embroidered robes, some add attractive beaded necklace and bracelet to their dressing while some employ the use of cowries to adorn their hair, clothes and many more. Unfortunately, these dresses have been replaced by clothing from other cultures, of which western culture being the most adopted dressing of them all.

Western clothing has predominated the dressing of Africans, and traditional wears have been reduced to occasional wears, of which this is also one of the implications of the influence made by other cultures on African culture.

Languages: Just as Africa is blessed with diverse dishes and clothing, Africa also has diverse languages, with more than 2,000 distinct languages, which are one-third of the world's language. Before colonization and before the immigrants came to Africa, the people of Africa are known to communicate in their respective indigenous languages, and the children were able to learn and speak the language fluently. Although there was no general language for the Africans in those days, this did not stop the people from co-existing peacefully.

It was up until people with other cultures from different continents began to migrate to Africa that the need to have a general language to communicate became imminent. Different languages were learned, but the most prominent of them all was the English language.

A vast number of Africans today choose the English language instead of their ancestral language, which gradually leads to the loss of the traditional heritage of their indigenous language. This influence is so great that all sectors in Africa now communicates in English. This influence has made a positive impact on the Africans in that it has broken the communication barrier between communities and countries, and it has also made a negative impact considering the rate at which Africans have adopted the new language and neglected their ancestral languages.

African Music and Entertainment: Music is a natural phenomenon in Africa, ranging from lullabies for infants to the songs of games for children down to the music and dances associated with adulthood.

This music is indigenous to Africa; they speak about the customs, responsibilities, beliefs, values, and rites of the community. They are usually accompanied by dance steps and musical instruments such as traditional drums, rattles, gongs, double bells, harps, djembes, and so on.

This music, dances, and all forms of entertainment done by the Africans in those days have significant meanings and interpretations, but unfortunately, this music has been replaced with English songs. The dancing steps are also on the verge of been forgotten. African musical instruments have been replaced with musical instruments from other cultures such as band-sets, saxophone, Electric drums, etc.

The earliest form of entertainment in Africa was through music, dancing, and playing of different traditional games, traditional plays, and storytelling where the community usually gather together in large groups to enjoy themselves; but now the influence of the western culture has made different means of entertainment available and accessible to everyone in the comfort of their home of which going out and bonding with your loved ones and society is not a criterion to be entertained as it was before the influence of other cultures.

Specific African Practices and beliefs: Due to civilization and influence of other cultures on the African culture, some of Africans religious, traditional practices and beliefs have been completely eroded. Some were good and beneficial practices while others were bad and harmful practices.

An example of harmful practices that was eroded as a result of the influence of other culture was the female genital mutilation which causes a lot of childbearing problems and infections for the young females in West Africa.

An example of the beneficial practices that have ceased among the Africans is the traditional rites for marriage, most cultures in those days follow some steps before conducting any marriage, and this is usually to ensure the safety of their children after leaving their custody. This practice has been neglected and no longer holds among the present time Africans.

4. Education and Technology

The impact of other cultures on African culture is also eminent in the development of the educational system and technological advancement of the continent.

The western influence has tremendously increased the lifestyle of Africans through technology advancement in different areas such as Agriculture, Medicine, Tourist centers, Natural resources, Transport systems, and so on.

Before the influence of other cultures, particularly the Westerners, the only form of education a child gets is the informal education, which is gotten from the parent and the environment around the child. Civilization and the influence of westerners have created a formal Educational system where children can get access to learn different subjects outside his/her family and environment and become useful in life.

Also, premature death and sickness attributed to natural disasters and angry gods were a norm in Africa before the influence of the other cultures. The only form of medicine they had were herbs and plants of which some of them were harmful to the body. Most of the treatments were done by local doctors who have no knowledge about the science of the body. It was after the colonization, independence, and civilization of most African countries that they began to have access to healthcare knowledge and facilities of the westerners, which have greatly reduced the death and disease rate of the Africans.

African sculptures, arts, and crafts have served as a source of income to the continent, agricultural products and natural resources have also been monetized to improve the economy of each country in the continent, and this is a direct result of the influence of other cultures on the African culture.

Apart from the positive impacts of other cultures on the educational and technological advancement highlighted above, the influence of technological advancement and education has also exposed the Africans to cultures that are against their ancestral cultures.

Technological advancement in Africa has been said to promote immorality, violence, profanity among the youths in Africa. Research has shown that many occult practices and gangsterism that occur in some African Tertiary Institutions today are a result of the games, movies, and other technological devices that were introduced to the Africans by the westerners.

In a nutshell, it is obvious that other cultures have left a considerable amount of impact on the African way of life. There have been positive impacts, and there have also been negative impacts. Although no culture is static, all cultures, whether African or not, has experienced change at a certain point or the other, but there are some countries that are conservative about preserving their heritage. An example is aFrench government, which forbids the use of English as the commercial language in the country despite the changes that have occurred in other countries.

In other to avoid the extinction of cultural and traditional values of Africa, there is a need to ensure cultural value rehabilitation in all sectors of the continent and also reduce the influx rate of western influence and other culture's influence on the continent by promoting the indigenous culture.

Although there are few cultures in Africa that still maintained their cultural beliefs and practices, it is said that people without a culture are people with no identity. The culture serves as the unique identity that differentiates people in the world, but now that the world is globalized most cultures have forgotten their identities and adopted the new trending cultures.

Therefore, it is important for any country or continent who wants to preserve their ancestral heritage to curb the rate at which other cultures are influencing their communities.

Chapter 9

Conclusion

Myths are the stories that inform the African people and shape their mode of thinking and actions. Children are usually told certain stories that are believed to have given rise to the cultural norms, values, ideals, principles, mores, and traditions. Throughout African myths, there are stories of men (heroes) who rose to become legends through their actions, which protected or saved the people of their time, such as Bayajida. There are also myths in which animals are the protagonists, such as Anansi.

There are many different countries in Africa, having varied cultural and ethnic groups and languages. The countries in Africa – although independent today – were at a time, colonies of the countries in Europe. Also, during the period of the Trans-Atlantic Slave Trade, many ports in Africa were the locations where slaves were bought and sold. Among those ports were Cairo in Egypt, Lagos in Nigeria, and the Cape in South Africa.

However, before the commencement of the slave trade or even colonization, many foreigners have migrated to African countries for various reasons, one of which is a search for better living conditions. For instance, the Turkish had been migrating to Egypt long before the slave trade began, and as a result, Egypt became an Islamic nation as the Turkish were

Muslims. In the case of Nigeria, migrants were usually from other African countries like Ghana, Benin, and Chad. Immigrants into South Africa before the slave trade began were from the Netherlands, France, Great Britain, Germany, Ireland, and Portugal.

Africa was majorly an agricultural continent before the coming of the Europeans. The major occupations were farming and hunting. The materials worn as clothes were usually made of leather, and the only places that were covered were places around the genitals – for both men and women.

Many countries in Africa have different gods (deities), which they believe are the sources of all that exists, and there are over a dozen gods from African nations. The African people worship these deities in one way or another, giving offerings and sacrifices in the hope that these deities will bless them, their families, and their lands.

Africa is a continent that is very rich in culture, and the myths, legends, gods, and goddesses of the various cultural groups are what make the nation great. If you visit a country, specifically a cultural group in Africa, try to familiarize yourself with its people, and you'll be amazed at the many things you will learn.

Do you know that I have also an audiobook series exclusively on Audible?

Scan here to find out more!

Book 2

ANCIENT AFRICAN KINGDOMS

From the Kingdom of Kush to the Mali Empire, Discover the History of Classical African Civilizations

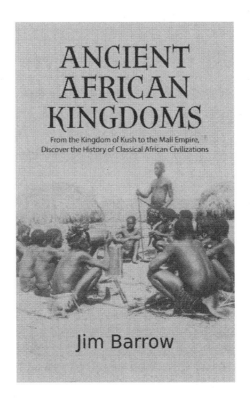

Chapter 1

List of kingdoms in precolonial africa

According to Vansina (1962), the five categories in which the sub-Saharan kingdoms in Africa (that is, Central Africa, South Africa, East Africa, and West Africa) were classified is given as follows:

- **Despotic Kingdoms**: These are kingdoms in which the rulers directly control both internal as well as external matters. Some of the kingdoms in this category include Ankole, the Kingdom of Kongo, and Rwanda.

- **Regal Kingdoms**: In regal kingdoms, the ruler is only responsible for handling external matters while the internal matters of the kingdom are handled by overseers. Usually, the chiefs and the king are a part of the same group and have the same religious beliefs.

- **Incorporative Kingdoms**: In these kingdoms, the ruler only handles matters that are external to the kingdom. He does not possess a lasting administrative connection to the chiefs, who are responsible for governing the provinces under the kingdom. Even after conquests, the regions governed by the chiefs of those provinces were not tampered with. Examples of such kingdoms are the Lunda and Luba Empires.

- **Aristocratic Kingdoms**: The paying of tribute was the only connection that the ruler of these kingdoms had with the provinces under them. Based on morphology, these kingdoms lie between regal kingdoms and federations.
- **Federations**: In these kingdoms, the matters that are external are handled by a council of elders, which is led by the ruler. An example of these kingdoms is the Ashanti Empire.

The kingdoms on this list are kingdoms that existed before the colonial periods in Africa. They fall into time periods in history referred to as "ancient," "post-classical," and "modern." Ancient history talks about the period when records of events in writing began, which is from 3600 BCE, more or less. Ancient history ended around 500 CE, in which period many great empires fell, including the Western Roman Empire in the Mediterranean, the Gupta Empire in India, and the Han Dynasty in China.

The post-classical era is the era between 500 CE to 1500 BCE in which events like the travels of Christopher Columbus and the conquest of Constantinople by the Ottoman Empire occurred. While modern history is the period where a more global network was created in the world, that is, when Europeans came in contact with Americans.

Precolonial Kingdoms of North Africa

Egyptian Empire

The Egyptian Empire, also called the New Kingdom, has been in existence for many years; however, the period between the 16th and 11th century BCE was the period when the kingdom enjoyed more prosperity throughout its existence. During the Second Intermediate Period (17th century), Kushites kept attacking the New Kingdom, and so in response, it expanded its territories into Nubia as well as the Near East.

After the death of Rameses III, three of his sons went on to become Pharaoh as Rameses IV, Rameses VI, and Rameses VIII. The kingdom suffered under droughts, flooding of the Nile, famine, civil unrest, and corrupt officers.

Kingdom of Kerma

Kerma kingdom was a kingdom in Kerma, Sudan. The kingdom flourished between 2500 and 1500 BCE, being the dominant kingdom in the region of Nubia from 2450 to 1450 BCE. The kingdom was established in Upper Nubia, currently occupied by modern-day northern and central Sudan; afterward, the kingdom's territory extended to Lower Nubia and to the Egyptian border. The kingdom stood against Egypt between 1700 and 1500 BCE; around 1500 BCE, it was incorporated into the New Kingdom (Kingdom of Egypt).

Carthaginian Empire

The Carthaginian Empire was a powerful empire that exercised dominance over the western Mediterranean until the middle of the 3rd century BCE. The capital of the empire was called Carthage, founded in 814 BCE. The empire was a cosmopolitan one, and it engaged Rome in a lot of battles called the Punic Wars between 264 and 146 BCE, threatening its power; it was in 146 BCE that Rome finally defeated the empire and forced all the states in Phoenicia under the empire to abide by Roman rule.

Kingdom of Blemmyes

The Blemmyes are people who Greeks, Romans, and Egyptians believed to have emerged from the Eastern Desert. These people occupied Lower Nubia in the latter part of the 4th century, and there, they founded a kingdom. The kingdom had a lot of important cities whose walls were made of combined Egyptian, Hellenic, Roman, and Nubian components – these cities include Faras, Ballama, and Aniba. Although sources say that the kingdom was not centralized; instead, the tribal cities came together in a kind of hierarchy. After the rulers, the next officials in the hierarchy were the phylarchs (chiefs).

Ptolemaic Kingdom

The Ptolemaic Kingdom was a Hellenic state founded in Egypt in ancient times. This kingdom was established in 350 BCE by a companion of Alexander the Great, Ptolemy I Soter. The kingdom existed up until 30 BCE, when Cleopatra passed away. The kingdom extended from eastern Libya to the Sinai and south to Nubia. The rulers of the kingdom took on the title of Pharaoh and asked artisans to portray their images on monuments in the styles and dresses of Egyptians so as to be accepted by Egyptian natives. The kingdom started waning due to strife between dynasties and foreign wars, which led it to rely heavily on the Roman Republic.

Kingdom of Kush

Kush was an antediluvian kingdom in the region of Nubia. The kingdom was founded along the Valley of the Nile, an area where modern-day northern Sudan and southern Egypt occupy. Egyptians identified the Kerma people as "Kush," and for many centuries, both Egypt and Kush engaged each other in sporadic trade, cultural exchange, and warfare. Many kingdoms in the Nubian region fell under the rule of the Kingdom of Egypt (1550 BCE to 1070 BCE); even though the Kushites built up a connection with the New Kingdom and they even had intermarriages, their culture was still different. During the time of the Late Bronze Age collapse, the Kush people went on to establish another kingdom in Napata, an area which is present-day Karima, Sudan.

Kingdom of Numidia

The Kingdom of Numidia was an antediluvian kingdom that was located in present-day Algeria, and its territories also spanned to touch a part of Tunisia as well as Libya in the Maghreb. In the beginning, the kingdom was split into two tribes; these tribes were the Massylii, which was in the east, and the Masaesyli in the west. However, King Masinissa of the Massyli overcame Syphax of the Masaesyli during the Punic Wars (218 BCE to 201 BCE) and united Numidia into a single kingdom. To the west, the kingdom shared a border with the Kingdom of Mauretania, to the east with the Moulouya River, Africa Proconsularis (currently a part of Tunisia), to the north with the Mediterranean Sea, and to the south with the Sahara. Numidia is seen to be one of the first significant kingdoms in the Berber world and Algeria's history. This great kingdom met its end as a result of the civil war that existed between Caesar and Pompey in 46 BCE.

Kingdom of Makuria

Makuria is another kingdom in the region of Nubia; it was located in modern-day northern Sudan and southern Egypt. In the first instance, the kingdom spanned over the region of the River Nile, beginning from the Third Cataract down to the south of Abu Hamad, and even down to northern Kordofan. The name of the kingdom's capital was Dongola. The culture of this kingdom developed more between the 9th and 11th century; in the 13th and 14th century, however, the kingdom waned due to several reasons such as increased Egyptian hostility, internal discord, Bedouin invasions, and the shifting of trade routes such that the empire was reduced to rubble, losing most of its territories in the south.

Kingdom of Nobatia

Nobatia or Nobadia is an ancient kingdom that was in Lower Nubia. Nobatia, Makuria, and Alodia combined to succeed the kingdom of Kush. The kingdom was founded in c. 400 and its territory was extended through the conquest of Blemmyes in the north; the kingdom then annexed the Blemmyes lands between the Second and Third Nile Cataract in the south. The kingdom adopted Coptic Christianity in c. 543, and by the 7th century, it was annexed into Makuria.

Kingdom of the Vandals and Alans

The Vandal kingdom is also known as the Kingdom of the Vandals and Alans; it was founded by the people of the Germanic Vandal. The period of the kingdom's predominance in North Africa and the Mediterranean is between c. 435 to c. 534. In the year c. 429, the Vandal peoples traveled over the ocean to North Africa from Hispania, and heading east on their journey, they subjugated the regions of present-day Morocco, Algeria, and Tunisia. The kingdom further overcame Carthage and the islands of Sicily, Sardinia, Corsica, and Mallorca, which were under Roman rule, challenging Roman authority, and the Romans retaliated by launching hostile expeditions unto the kingdom, which failed. In 534, Belisarius defeated the kingdom in the Vandalic War and annexed it into the Eastern Roman Empire, also referred to as the Byzantine Empire.

Kingdom of Nekor

The kingdom of Nekor was a domain that was located in modern-day Morocco, precisely the Rif region, and, the emirate was established in the year c. 710. The capital of the emirate was originally set at Temsaman before it was later moved to Nekor. The kingdom was subjugated under a group of Vikings in the year 859; these Vikings defeated the Moors' army in Nekor that tried to disturb their plunder in the region. The Vikings departed Morocco after eight days and headed for Spain.

Fatimid Caliphate

The Fatimid Caliphate was a caliphate of the 10th to 12th century CE; it covered a huge area of land in North Africa, beginning at the Red Sea, which was toward the east and to the west toward the Atlantic Ocean. The heart of the caliphate was Egypt, and the other regions that were part of the caliphate were Sudan, Sicily, the Levant, Maghreb, and the

Hijaz. In the year 921, the Fatimid people moved their capital to Mahdia, a city of Tunisia.

Spanning from the late 11th century through to the 15th century, the caliphate dwindled ever so swiftly; with the coming of the year 1171, the territory of the caliphate was invaded by Saladin, who annexed it into the Abbasid Caliphate.

Almohad Caliphate

Almohad Caliphate was a Muslim kingdom of the Berbers in North Africa that was established during the 12th century. At the pinnacle of the empire's existence, much of the Iberian Peninsula and the Maghreb in North Africa were under its control. The empire continued to exercise authority over Iberia until Christian princes of Castile, Aragon, and Navarre formed an alliance in order to defeat Muhammad III "al-Nasir," who was overcome in Sierra Morena during the Battle of Las Navas de Tolosa (1199 to 1214).

Territories belonging to the Moors were lost after that battle, including Cordova and Seville. Soon after, the caliphate began to lose its territories bit by bit as various tribes and districts started revolting, thus enabling the Marinids (Banu Marin), who were the most effective of their enemies.

Mamluk Sultanate

The Mamluk Sultanate was an empire that made itself into a caliphate; it had land covering Egypt, the Levant, and Hejaz. The empire lasted from the period where the Ayyubid dynasty was overthrown through to the conquest of Egypt by the Ottomans in 1517. The rule of Mamluk is broken down into two periods: the first is referred to as the "Turkic" period, while the second is the "Circassian" period. The pinnacle of the empire's existence was during the Turkic rule, but the Circassian period came with a stage of its decline. A contributory factor to this decline was the reduction in revenues to the Mamluk-Venetian monopoly on the trans-Mediterranean trade caused by the expansion of the Portuguese empire into Africa and Asia.

Kingdom of Tlemcen

The kingdom of Tlemcen was a kingdom in the northwestern part of present-day Algeria; the kingdom's area of land spanned through Tlemcen to the Chelif bend and Algiers. The kingdom further stretched to the Moulouya River to the west, to the south, it reached the Sijilmasa and down east, to the Soummam River. A lack of geographical unity, internal disputes, a lack of fixed frontiers, and dependence on the Arabs for military troops were some of the reasons that led to the fall of the kingdom.

Marinid Sultanate

The Marinid Sultanate was a kingdom that existed between the 13th century to the 15th century that ruled over modern-day Morocco as well as other areas like Algeria and Tunisia in North Africa and southern Spain and Gibraltar. The empire's name was derived from a Zenata tribe of the Berbers known as Banu Marin. A sequence of the rapid takeover of rulership by each Sultan beginning in the year 1358, a division of the empire, and political anarchy were the series of events that set the stage leading to the complete destruction of the empire.

Republic of Salé

The Republic of Salé was a city-state that was established along the Bou Regreg river at Salé; it was a kingdom that was established in the 17th century by Moriscos from a town known as Hornachos in the western part of Spain. Moriscos were people of Muslim descent who were Christian converts by title and were victims of the mass deportation at the time of the Spanish Inquisition. The city is now a part of the kingdom of Morocco.

Precolonial Kingdoms of East Africa

Kingdom of Punt

The kingdom of Punt was an antediluvian kingdom that produced gold, aromatic resins, blackwood, ebony, ivory, and wild animals; the kingdom traded with the ancient kingdom of Egypt. The kingdom had lands that stretched through the Horn of Africa to southern Arabia; believed to be located toward the southeast of Egypt and covering littoral of present-day northeast Ethiopia, Djibouti, Somalia, Eritrea, the Red Sea, and Sudan.

Kingdom of Begwena

The kingdom of Begwena was a kingdom of North Africa in the early part of the Middle Ages with what is now northern Ethiopia as the heart of its empire; back then, the center of the kingdom was called Lalibela. The kingdom controlled land that stretched up to nearly 800 miles.

Kingdom of D'mt

D'mt was an empire that was located in Eritrea and the Tigray Region (northern Ethiopia). It was in existence between the 10th century and 5th century BCE. However, not much is known about the kingdom as there are only a few surviving inscriptions and scant archeological work has been undertaken.

Harla Kingdom

This was a kingdom that existed in the 6th century that had what is now eastern Ethiopia as the heart of its empire. It traded with both the Ayyubid and Tang dynasties; it had land spanning between just over 500 yards east to west and almost 1,000 yards north to south. One study of the ancient kingdom shows that the people used knives; thus, their culture was common with that of the Islamic world of Arabia, Mesopotamia, the Levant, and Iberia.

Kingdom of Bazin

Bazin was an ancient kingdom of the medieval period with the heart of its empire in East Africa. The kingdom was among the six states in existence in the 9th century. The lands of the kingdom were based in between Aswan and Massawa.

Kingdom of Semien

Semien was an ancient kingdom that was also referred to as the Kingdom of Beta Israel; the heart of the kingdom was located in the northwestern part of the Ethiopian Empire. The kingdom ended in the year 1627 under the rule of Susenyos I after it engaged the Ethiopian empire in war and was conquered.

Kingdom of Kitara | Chwezi

The Kitara Empire, also called the Chwezi Empire, is the kingdom of the Bakitara people, which had dominance over territories stretching through the valley of the Nile and beyond. After the kingdom of Aksum broke into Makuria, Zagwe, Shewa, and Damot kingdoms in East Africa, a kingdom that broke into the south was the Kitara Empire. After a prophecy of the empire's demise came, many believed it; after an invasion into the empire, its people dispersed into Rwanda, Burundi, Ankole, and Eastern Congo.

Kilwa Sultanate

The Kilwa Sultanate was an ancient empire in medieval times that had Kilwa – an island outside modern-day Tanzania – as the heart of the empire. The empire is said to have been established by a Persian prince of Shiraz by the name of Ali ibn al-Hassan Shirazi. The kingdom went into decline when the Portuguese began to interfere with its rule beginning in the year 1500.

Kingdom of Medri Bahri

The kingdom of Medri Bahri was an antediluvian kingdom that occupied modern-day Eritrea that existed from the 12th century to the time it was taken over by Ethiopians. Once an independent kingdom, Medri Bahri was made to pay tributes to the Ethiopian Empire until the Ethiopian empire finally incorporated it into its kingdom.

Ethiopian Empire

Abyssinia, or as it is more popularly known, the Ethiopian Empire, was an empire that covered the territory of what is now Ethiopia and Eritrea. Its existence began in the 11th century, being established by Yekuno Amlak and up to 1974 when Haile Selassie, the then ruler of the kingdom was subverted in a coup d'état. The kingdom fought many wars to preserve its territory especially with the Italian Empire; however, it lost, and the Italian Empire occupied it and established a colony of Italian East Africa in the area. Although the Ethiopian empire incorporated Eritrea into it in 1962, a civil war broke out in the empire causing Eritrea to gain independence and subsequently leading to the fall of the Ethiopian empire.

Sultanate of Ifat

The Sultanate of Ifat was a Muslim empire that existed between the 13th century through the 15th century in the east region of East Africa. The heart of the empire was a city called Zeila. The territories of the kingdom include eastern Ethiopia, Djibouti, and Somaliland of the modern day. In the early part of the 15th century, Emperor Dawit I defeated the then ruler of the empire and then destroyed the kingdom.

Hadiya Sultanate

The Hadiya Sultanate was an antediluvian empire that was based in southwestern Ethiopia; from the Abbay River, it is located south, and from Shewa, it is to the west. The land was fertile, its people grew cereals and fruits and owned horses, and iron was the empire's currency.

Sultanate of Mogadishu

The Mogadishu Sultanate is also called the Kingdom of Magadazo, and it was an ancient empire that was based in southern Somalia. It rose to be one of the empires to dominate the region of East Africa when it was being ruled by Fakhr ad-Din before it was incorporated into the Ajuran Empire in the 13th century. It had a large network of trade and had its own currency.

Kingdom of Buganda

Buganda kingdom is a kingdom of the Ganda people of Uganda, and it is the largest of the kingdoms in East Africa today. Before the 12th century, the kingdom was known as Muwaawa. However, the kingdom lost its independence to British rule and its adopted name became Uganda, which is the Swahili translation of Buganda. It regained its independence in 1962. It still is in existence today and is ruled by Queen Sylvia Nagginda.

Ajuran Sultanate

The Ajuran Empire was an empire in ancient times belonging to the Muslim Sultanate of Somalia which exercised dominance over East Africa. The government of the Sultanate was centralized, and it had a strong military to oppose foreign invasions. The empire was invested in architecture as it built castles and fortresses. The empire started to dwindle toward the end of the 17th century and this led to the rise of other Somalian powers.

Kingdom of Kaffa

The Kaffa Kingdom was an empire that was based in present-day Ethiopia, having Bonga as its offset capital. The kingdom had different groups of people living within its borders, such as the hunters called *Manje*, the leatherworkers, known as the *Manne*, and the blacksmiths called *Qemmo*. The kingdom was overcome and incorporated by Ethiopia in the year 1897.

Kingdom of Rwanda

The Rwanda Kingdom was a Bantu kingdom in the Horn of Africa that existed before colonial rule. Though it fell under the rule of German and Belgian colonists, it retained its monarchical system of government until the 1961 Rwandan Revolution.

Adal Sultanate

The Kingdom of Adal, also known as the Adal Sultanate, was a Muslim kingdom and Sultanate of Somalia in East Africa. The kingdom was founded by local people who occupied Zeila, and it attained its greatest height between 1415 to 1577. The empire lost the majority of its lands after the death of its ruler, Imam Ahmed; its fall resulted from internal disputes within the Afar tribes.

Ankole Kingdom

The Ankole kingdom was an antediluvian Bantu kingdom that was based in southwestern Uganda and faced Lake Edward from the east. Mugabe (Omugabe) was the name of the kingdom's ruler. The kingdom was annexed into the British Protectorate of Uganda.

Kingdom of Burundi

The kingdom of Burundi was an empire that was located in what is today the Republic of Burundi, in East Africa, precisely the region of the Great Lakes. The kingdom was established in the 17th century and it fell under the rulership of European colonists in the 19th century.

Kingdom of Kooki

Kooki was a traditional empire located in the modern-day Rakai District of Uganda. The year 1720 was the year the kingdom was established by two Bunyoro princes whose names were Bwowe and Kitayimbwa. It was annexed into the Buganda Kingdom in 1896.

Sultanate of the Geledi

The Geledi Sultanate was an empire that had dominance over East Africa in the latter part of the 17th century and the 19th century. At its height, the kingdom built up an army under the rulership of Mahmud Ibrahim, who was the Sultan of that time.

Sultanate of Aussa

The Sultanate of Aussa was a kingdom that was in eastern Ethiopia, precisely in the region of Afar between the 18th century and the 19th century. This empire was believed to be the leading monarchy of the people of Afar. In 1936, it was annexed into Italian East Africa.

Majeerteen Sultanate

The Majeerteen Sultanate was a kingdom of the Somalian people; it was based in East Africa. The sultanate exercised dominance over the majority of northern Somalia in the latter part of the 19th century and early 20th century.

Kingdom of Gomma

The kingdom of Gomma was a kingdom in the Gibe area of Ethiopia that rose to prominence in the 18th century. The heart of the kingdom was Agaro, bordered to the north by Limmu-Ennarea, to the west by Gumma, the south by Gera, and the east by Jimma.

Tooro Kingdom

A section of the Bunyoro people broke out of the Bunyoro kingdom, and those people finally established a kingdom of their own known as the Kingdom of Tooro in the 19th century, precisely in the year 1830. In 1876, the kingdom was annexed into Bunyoro-Kitara; however, it regained its independence in 1891.

Kingdom of Jimma

Jimma was among the kingdoms in the region of Gibe in Ethiopia that rose to prominence in the 19th century. It was bordered to the west by Limmu-Ennarea, to the east by the Sidamo Kingdom of Janjero; and to the south, the Gojeb River stood between the empire and the Kingdom of Kaffa.

Kingdom of Gumma

Gumma was a kingdom from the Gibe region in Ethiopia that rose to prominence in the 18th century. It shared its eastern borders with the bend of the Didessa River that stood between it and Limmu-Ennarea, which was located toward the northeast, and Gomma and Gera kingdoms toward the south.

Sultanate of Hobyo

The Sultanate of Hobyo was a kingdom of the people of Somalia located in northeastern and central Somalia and eastern Ethiopia of today. Yusuf Ali Kenadid founded the kingdom in 1807; he was the cousin of the Sultan of the Majeerteen Sultanate.

Kingdom of Karagwe

Karagwe was a kingdom that was part of the kingdoms of the Great Lakes in the Horn of Africa. It achieved prominence in the early part of the 19th century under the rulership of King Ndagara.

Kingdom of Unyanyembe

The kingdom of Unyanyembe was a kingdom that was established in the 19th century. The kingdom had two capital cities, which were Tabora and Kwihara. The empire had to endure the fight for power between Mnywasela and Mkasiwa.

Precolonial Kingdoms of West Africa

Kingdom of Ife

The Kingdom of Ife, also referred to as Ilé-Ifé, is an ancient kingdom in the southwest of Nigeria; it is currently located in Osun State. Ancient artwork from the kingdom, such as sculptures of stone, terracotta, and bronze, show that the kingdom existed around 1200 CE.

Kingdom of Nri

The Nri Kingdom was a kingdom located in present-day Nigeria. One-third of Igboland were under the political and religious rule of the kingdom, and the ruler of the kingdom was a priest-king bearing the title *Eze Nri*. The ruler handled both trade and diplomatic matters relating to the people, and he possessed divine authority in the sphere of religion. The influence of the kingdom waned with the rise of the Benin Empire.

Takrur

Takrur was an ancient kingdom in West Africa that was established in c. 800. The period of prosperity in the kingdom was sometime around the time the Ghana Empire also boomed. In 1235, the kingdom started declining and was eventually overcome by the Mali Empire in the 1280s.

Bonoman

Bonoman was an Akan kingdom in ancient times. The kingdom was based in modern-day southern Ghana – specifically the Bono, Bono East, and Ahafo areas – and eastern Ivory Coast. Many believe it to be the place where the subgroups of Akan people originated. The rise of other Akan kingdoms brought about its downfall, especially since its people started deserting the kingdom.

Benin Empire

The kingdom of Benin was an ancient kingdom of West Africa located in modern-day southern Nigeria. The modern-day nation-state called Benin and this empire are different. The capital of the kingdom was Edo; currently, it is called Benin City in Edo State. It was established in the 11th century CE, and it stood until 1897 when it was incorporated into the British Empire.

Oyo Empire

The Oyo Empire was a kingdom located in present-day Benin and Western Nigeria; its territory spanned the whole of southwestern Nigeria and the western part of northcentral Nigeria. It was the largest state of the Yoruba people and one of the significant kingdoms of West Africa from the middle of the 7th century to the late 18th century.

Kingdom of Dagbon

Dagbon Kingdom was an ancient kingdom in Ghana, established by the Dagomba (Dagamba) people in the 11th century. During the prominent period of the kingdom's existence, its territory covered the Northern, Upper West, and Upper East areas of what is now Ghana.

Sultanate of Agadez

The Sultanate of Agadez was a kingdom of the Berbers based in the city of Agadez which is located on the southern borders of the Sahara Desert in the north-central part of Niger. The kingdom was founded in 1449 by the Tuareg and Hausa people to serve as a country store. The kingdom faced decline in both economic activity and population in the 17th century and finally, was conquered by the French in 1900.

Mamprugu Kingdom

This kingdom was founded in the 13th century by Naa Gbanwah at Pusiga, which is away from Bawku with only a few miles' distance. Its territories include the North-East, Northern, Upper East, and Upper West regions of Ghana and down to Burkina Faso.

Kwararafa Confederacy

Kwararafa Confederacy was a state having different ethnic groups that were based around the valley of the Benue River in present-day Nigeria. It was established to the southwest of the Bornu Empire; the kingdom became prominent before the year 1500. By the 17th century, the kingdom had various conflicts with neighboring kingdoms and declined to become a tributary in the 18th century.

Kingdom of Cayor

The Kingdom of Cayor was the most influential kingdom in West Africa between the years 1549 and 1879. It broke off from the Jolof Empire in present-day Senegal. The kingdom was incorporated into the French Empire twice, first in 1868 and then again in 1879.

Kingdom of Dahomey

The kingdom of Dahomey was an African kingdom located in what is now the nation-state of Benin. The kingdom was founded in the early part of the 17th century, developing on the Plateau of Abomey amidst the Fon people. It was incorporated into the French colonial empire in 1904.

Wukari Federation

Wukari is a traditional land that succeeded Kwararafa. The kingdom currently lies in the south of the Benue River Basin, in Taraba State, Nigeria. The Jukun people came to settle in Wukari in the 17th century.

Asante Empire

The Asante Empire was an empire of the Akan people that was established in the late 17th century of what is now Ghana. The kingdom's territory stretched from Ashanti to include the Brong-Ahafo Region, Central Region, Eastern Region, and Western Region of modern-day Ghana. It fell when it became part of the Gold Coast colony in 1902.

Kong Empire

The Kong Empire was an ancient kingdom that was established by the Dyula immigrants from the Mali Empire, which was declining at the time. The kingdom became prominent in the 1800s. The kingdom fell when it suffered an attack from Samori Ture in 1898.

Precolonial Kingdoms of Central Africa

Kingdom of Kongo

Kongo was a kingdom that was located in Central Africa in what is now northern Angola, the western region of DR Congo, the Republic of Congo, and the deep south of Gabon. At its height, the kingdom's territories spanned in the west from the Atlantic Ocean to the Kwango River in the east, and in the north from the Congo River to the Kwanza River in the south.

Sultanate of Bagirmi

The Sultanate of Bagirmi was a kingdom in the southeast of Lake Chad in Central Africa. The kingdom was established in either the year 1480 or the year 1552; the kingdom's capital city was Massenya that was to the north of the Chari River and near the border of modern-day Cameroon. The kingdom was incorporated into the Wadai Sultanate in 1871.

Luba Empire

The Luba Kingdom was a kingdom existing before Central Africa fell under colonial rule, established by King Kongolo Mwamba in roughly 1585. At the height of the empire, the king was receiving tribute from about one million people. The kingdom fell not long after it was raided by invaders in search of slaves.

Kingdom of Ndongo

The Ndongo Kingdom was a kingdom that occupied present-day Angola. Not much is known about the kingdom;

however, it was more or less a feudatory of the Kingdom of Kongo as suggested by oral tradition.

Anziku Kingdom

Another prior kingdom to colonial Central Africa was the Anziku Kingdom, also called the Teke Kingdom. The kingdom was located in what is now the Republic of Congo, Gabon, and the Democratic Republic of Congo. The Anziku people were in control of the copper mines in the northeast border of Kongo.

Kasanje Kingdom

The Kasanje Kingdom was established in the year 1620 by a band of mercenaries from Imbangala who had defected from the Portuguese army. The kingdom was named after the leader of the mercenaries; the people elected a king from one of the three clans that established the kingdom.

Kingdom of Matamba

The Matamba Kingdom was a kingdom that was in existence before the era of colonial Central Africa, located in a region currently called the Baixa de Cassanje of the Melanje Province of present-day Angola. This kingdom resisted the colonists of Portugal for many years before it was annexed into Angola.

Lunda Empire

Lunda kingdom was a kingdom whose ruler was called the Mwane-a- n'Gaange. At the pinnacle of its existence, the kingdom was in control of territories of about 186,000 square miles. Having great military strength, it conquered various tribes; however, it was invaded by the Chokwe in the 19th century, and the kingdom fell.

Kuba Kingdom

The Kuba Kingdom was a kingdom that started as a conglomerate of different Bushongo-speaking tribes; there was no central authority. However, in about 1625, Shyaam a-Mbul a Ngoong seized power from one of the tribe's leaders and then united the other tribes into one under his rule. The period of heyday in the kingdom was between the 17th century and the 19th century.

Mbunda Kingdom

The Kingdom of Mbunda was an empire that was based in present-day southeast Angola in west Central Africa. At its height, the kingdom had land that stretched from Mithimoyi in central Morocco to Cuando Cubango Province in the southeast, sharing a border with Namibia. It was conquered by Portugal in the year 1914 during the Kolongongo War.

Adamawa Emirate

The Adamawa Emirate was a kingdom that was based in Fombina, which is more or less the region of Adamawa and Taraba states in Nigeria today, the three northern provinces of Cameroon, some areas of Chad, and the Central African Republic. It was established by a commander of Usman dan Fodio by the name of Modibo Adama in 1809.

Yeke Kingdom

The Yeke Kingdom was a kingdom that did not stand for long, existing between 1856 to 1891. It is an empire of the people of Garanganze in Katanga, Democratic Republic of Congo. Although, in its short existence, it rose to prominence and had a territory that was around 300 million square miles.

Precolonial Kingdoms of South Africa

Mapungubwe Kingdom

The kingdom of Mapungubwe was a kingdom in South Africa that was located where the Shashe and Limpopo Rivers meet, south of Great Zimbabwe. The period of the kingdom's existence was around c. 1075 to c. 1220. It set the stage for development that eventually led to the establishment of the Kingdom of Zimbabwe.

Kingdom of Zimbabwe

The Kingdom of Zimbabwe was a Karanga or Shona kingdom that existed between c.1000 and c. 1450. The kingdom was located in modern-day Zimbabwe, and the name of its capital was Lusvingo; it emerged after the kingdom of Mapungubwe collapsed. Around 1430, Prince Nyatsimba Mutota left the kingdom to go establish a dynasty of his own; that dynasty rose to become the Kingdom of Mutapa, which eventually dominated the Kingdom of Zimbabwe.

Kingdom of Mutapa

The Mutapa Empire was a kingdom with land that spanned through present-day Zimbabwe, Zambia, Mozambique, and South Africa. A little after the establishment of the kingdom, its land stretched for most of the territories between Tavara and the Indian Ocean. The vulnerability of the kingdom to attack and economic manipulation, as well as internal disputes, led to the collapse of the kingdom.

Kingdom of Butua

The Kingdom of Butua was a kingdom located in modern-day southwestern Zimbabwe. It was a gold source for both Arab traders and traders from Portugal. The kingdom was in existence between c. 1450 and c. 1683.

Maravi Kingdom

The Maravi Kingdom was a kingdom that was established in the 3rd century. By the 16th century, it spanned across the borders of present-day Malawi, Mozambique, and Zambia. In its heyday, the lands of the kingdom stretched from the area of the Tonga and Tumbuka people (north) to the Lower Shire (south).

Merina Kingdom

The Kingdom of Merina, also known as the Kingdom of Madagascar, existed from c. 1540 to c. 1897. It was located outside the coast of Southeast Africa, and it exercised dominance over the majority of present-day Madagascar in the 19th century.

Rozvi Empire

The Rozvi Empire was established in 1684 on the Plateau of Zimbabwe around Changamire Dombo. A number of reasons led to the empire's collapse, including the hostility between the ruling dynasty and the allied kingdoms, which caused many to desert the empire; and, it suffered two major droughts from 1795 to 1800 and from 1824 to 1829.

Ndwandwe Kingdom

This was a kingdom whose people spoke Bantu-Nguni; combined with the Mthethwa, they became an important authority in Zululand of the modern-day by the 19th century. The kingdom was destroyed when its army was defeated at the Battle of Mblatuze River.

Mthethwa Empire

The Mthethwa Empire was a South African kingdom that rose to prominence in the 18th century from the south of Delagoa Bay and inland in southeast Africa. According to scholars, Nguni tribesmen descended from northern Natal and the Lubombo Mountains. The empire was replaced by the Zulu Kingdom.

Zulu Kingdom

The Kingdom of Zululand was a South African empire that stretched through the Indian Ocean coast from the Tugela River (south) to the Pongola River (north). In 1879, the kingdom exercised dominance over the majority of modern-day KwaZulu-Natal and Southern Africa. The kingdom fell to the British in the Battle of Ulundi.

Ndebele Kingdom

The Ndebele Kingdom was a kingdom in Southern Africa that was home to the Mthwakazi – the proto-Ndebele people. Bantu people arrived in the kingdom sometime later, and the kingdom became a place for the settlement of different cultures.

African kingdoms in the precolonial period also include the Sahelian kingdoms which are not included in this list. They are written under a different subtopic.

Chapter 2

The kingdom of kush

The Kingdom of Kush had its capital located in present-day Northern Sudan. Kush was a kingdom that formed from the much older region of Nubia that was already inhabited since c. 8,000 BCE and stretched from the upper Nile leading up to the Red Sea. The kingdom of Kush was instrumental in the political and cultural developments of the Northeastern part of Africa. The kingdom was in existence for over a thousand years.

The Kingdom of Kush was largely influenced by the Egyptians as archeological evidence from Egypt and Sudan proves that they in contact as far back as c. 3150 BCE to c. 2614 BCE. This was the earliest period of development of the Egyptian Dynasty. The earliest reference of Kush by the Egyptians was the attack on it led by the founder of the middle kingdom, Mentuhotep II, in the 21st century BCE. In fact, Kush, sometimes referred to as Nubia, was a colony under the rule of the new Kingdom of Egypt around the 16th century BCE. The colony of Kush was governed by an Egyptian viceroy. The Kingdom of Kush rose after the collapse of the Bronze Age and also the collapse of the new

Kingdom of Egypt in c. 1070 BCE and had its capital in Napata, which is located today in central Sudan.

The Kingdom of Kush, under the rule of King Kashta (also known as the Kushite), invaded Egypt in the 8th century. After the invasion, the Kushite kings would become pharaohs of the "Twenty-Fifth Dynasty" of Egypt. They ruled Egypt for one century and were later expelled in c. 656 BCE by the Psamtik. The capital of Kush Kingdom was later moved to Monroe, which according to Greek geographers was known as Aethiopia. It lasted until the 4th century CE before its disintegration caused by internal revolts. The kingdom is believed to be the most famous and long-lasting civilization that rose from Nubia, all through its existence of about three thousand years, and had its capital located in first Kerma, Napata, and lastly Meroe (or Monroe).

The kingdom of Kush was very wealthy, as every part of the kingdom contributed to its wealth. During its occupation by the Egyptians, Kush served as the main source of gold. Kush and later the Kingdom of Kush was called several names by different people. Because the region supplied gold to Egypt, some historians claimed that Nubia was derived from "nub," which is the Egyptian word for gold. Although the Egyptians also had another name for the region, which was Ta-Nehsy, meaning the "land of the black people." Kush was also referred to as "Aethiopia," which meant the "land inhabited by the people with a burnt face." And to the Arabs, it was known as Bilad al-Sudan, which meant "land of the black."

Kerma and Early Kush

The city of Kerma, which became the first capital of the kingdom of Kush, was founded in c. 2400 BCE. The city was built around a fortified religious center known as a "deffufa." It was built with mud bricks and had a height of fifty-nine feet. The worship center had several inner passageways alongside stairs that led to the altar located at the roof. This alter was where ceremonies were conducted, although little is known about the details of these ceremonies. There were smaller deffufa to the west and to the east (which is the smallest), and together, they formed a triad. This religious center triad became the center upon which the city was built and walls constructed around the city.

From Egyptian inscriptions and evidence of fortified buildings built to the south of Egypt to defend it against enemies, Kerma was an acknowledged rival. Despite this, there were trade relations between Kerma and Egypt. Egypt's influx of goods such as ebony, gold, incense, ivory, animals, and so forth, was dependent on imports from Kerma. The Kushites, together with the Hyksos and Egyptians, had a tripartite trade relation in the region of Thebes. These trade relations were ended by the invasion and expulsion of the Hyksos by the Egyptians, who felt threatened by the military might of the people. This expedition was led by Ahmose I, who ruled Egypt from c. 1570 BCE to 1544 BCE. After Hyksos, he turned his attention to the Kushites. Egypt's attack on the Kushites continued under the reign of both Thutmose I and Thutmose III, who ruled from 1520 to 1492 BCE and 1458 to 1425 BCE, respectively. After Thutmose III successfully defeated and sacked Kerma, he established the city of Napata to consolidate the power of Egypt in the entire region. C. 1500 BCE is generally held as the year Kerma collapsed.

Napata

As seen above, Napata was the creation of the Egyptians, and as such, from its onset, it was greatly influenced by Egyptian culture. Thutmose III, after establishing Napata, built close to the mountain of Jebel Barkal, the great temple of Amun. This temple became the most outstanding religious center throughout the history of the Kushites. Other Egyptian pharaohs, such as Ramesses II, contributed to the architecture of the temple. Subsequent autonomous Kushite kings were religiously under the control of the priests of Amun just the same way their former hegemony, Egyptian pharaohs, were since the era of the Old Kingdom.

The New Kingdom of Egypt began to decline in c. 1069. This decline was partly a result of the struggle for power between the priests of Amun and the pharaoh, which resulted in the separation of the kingdom's political administration. The priests of Amun at Thebes gained much power from c. 1069 to 525 BCE. This period was known as Egypt's Third Intermediate Period. During this period, Egypt was divided into Upper and Lower Egypt. The High Priest of Amun had political control of Upper Egypt while the pharaoh only had political control over Lower Egypt. As Egypt grew weak, Kush was gaining strength, and Napata gradually grew into an independent political entity. Egypt could no longer maintain its sovereignty over it as it had internal crises to deal with. Many scholars mark c. 1069 BCE as the birth date of the kingdom of Kush because it was when the Kushite rulers began to reign autonomously, free from interference from Egyptian politics or monarchs. Although the kingdom of Kush was now autonomous, they still maintained trade relations with Egypt and neighboring nations. But now, they dictated the terms as they saw fit. For quite some time, the royal necropolis remained in Kerma, the kingdom's first capital, and kings had to be buried there until it was moved to Napata. The kingdom of Kush grew mightily to the point of having the powers to oppress its former oppressors. But every time they would enter Egypt it was to preserve and defend Egyptian culture and not to conquer it. A typical example was the Twenty-Fifth Dynasty.

The Twenty-Fifth Dynasty

King Alara took advantage of the opportunity presented by the decline in Egyptian power and wealth during the Third Intermediate Period. He unified the kingdom under the capital of Napata. Although there are no documented dates for him, he was a very popular king among the people of Kush. Evidence of his rule can be found in inscriptions that were discovered on what appears to be his tomb. He laid a very good foundation for his successor Kashta. Under Kashta's reign, Napata and the entire kingdom of Kush was "Egyptianized." He imported numerous Egyptian artifacts for decoration and religious purposes to the kingdom.

Kashta had a very good relationship with the priests of Amun in Thebes who controlled Upper Egypt. He capitalized on this relationship and had his daughter, who was named Amenirdis I, chosen as the wife of the gods. The wife of the gods is a position held by a woman who had the same political powers and wealth as the High Priest of Amun. This was a very important position in Egyptian society. All of this was made possible because of the persistent decline of the powers of the pharaoh after losing their rule over Upper Egypt. Kashta then used his daughter to usurp the powers of the High Priest and gained control of Thebes. With control over Thebes, he seized control over the whole of Upper

Egypt. Again, the princes who were fighting among themselves could not interfere. With his daughter controlling Upper Egypt and disunity among members of the ruling class in Lower Egypt, Kashta declared himself king of all Egypt. He was successful and established what is now called in history the Twenty-Fifth Dynasty of Egypt without using military force. Piye, who was Kashta's son, succeeded him from c. 747 to 721 BCE.

When Piye ascended the throne, he enforced Kushite rule over Upper and Lower Egypt. Though he met little resistance from the princes who were weak and divided, he deployed his army and subdued every city in Lower Egypt. After establishing his sovereignty, he then returned home to Napata. He restored existing kings and consolidated their authority to rule as it has always been. The only thing Piye requested was for them to recognize him as "lord." Piye never occupied Egypt. At his death, his brother Shabaka became king from c. 721 to 707 BCE, and he continued in his brother's footsteps. Shabaka also allowed the indigenous kings of Egypt to maintain their autonomy so long as they recognized his sovereignty. Like his brother, he too remained and ruled from the capital of Kush, Napata. Shabaka was also a lover of the Egyptian culture like his brother and father before him. During his rule, it is believed that the "Egyptianization" of the kingdom was so deep to the extent that when King Shabaka marched into Lower Egypt to suppress the rebellion of the princes and finally imposed the Nubian culture on the Egyptians, scholars say he was only still imposing Egyptian culture on the Egyptians. Shabaka consolidated his rule by making Haremakhet, his son, appointed as the High Priest of Amun. Shabaka, contrary to some beliefs, preserved Egyptian culture.

Shabaka was succeeded by Shebitku, his nephew from c. 707 to 690 BCE. Under his reign, the kingdom of Kush and its colony Egypt continued to flourish. Shebitku, like his uncle, continued to give asylum to rebel leaders who escaped Assyria in Mesopotamia. For example, the kingdom of Kush gave sanctuary to Ashdod, the leader of the revolution against King Sargon of Assyria. This caused the Assyrians to attack Egypt in 671 BCE during the reign of Shebitku's successor, King Taharqa. King Taharqa was defeated, captured and taken to Nineveh alongside his family and other Kushite and Egyptian royals. King Taharqa escaped to Napata. Tantamani succeeded him from c. 669 BCE to 666 BCE, and continued to support rebels against Assyria. Egypt was finally conquered in 666 BCE, and this ended the Twenty-Fifth Dynasty.

City of Meroe

After the Assyrians defeated the king of the Kingdom of Kush and took over Egypt, they placed over its affairs Pharaoh Necho I, who was succeeded by Psamtik I, his son, from 665 to 610 BCE. During the reign of Psamtik, Egypt was liberated from the Assyrians. This marked the beginning of the Twenty-Sixth Dynasty. After his death, Necho II succeeded him, and he led an attack on the Kingdom of Kush. Pharaoh Necho II sacked Kush's capital city of Napata as well as other towns, monuments, temples, and so forth, and although Necho II was successful, he did not occupy the kingdom but pulled back his troops and returned to Egypt. In c. 590 BCE, after the destruction of Napata, the King of Kush moved the capital of the kingdom to a city called Meroe. In Meroe, the Kingdom of Kush continued to follow the same culture, religion, and administrative system as the Egyptians. But when Arkamana I ascended the throne in c. 295 BCE and ruled until 275 BCE, he refuted the Egyptian customs and pattern of administration. It is believed that the king was schooled in Greek philosophy, hence he decided to do away with the absurd beliefs of the people that were upheld by the priests of Amun. Hitherto, the priests of Amun ultimately controlled the Kings of Kush the same way it was in the Egyptian society. The priests had the power to change the monarch and force the former to commit suicide. This, the High Priest did by merely declaring the gods did not want the ruler anymore. Arkamani I abolished the priest's powers over the kings by killing all the priests of Amun.

During the reign of Arkamani I, the Kingdom of Kush saw the institution of new practices and customs different to and independent of those practiced in Egypt. The kingdom found its own identity under Arkamani I. Among the things that changed was the hitherto Egyptian fashion style to Meroitic fashion, hieroglyphic script to Meroitic script. Also, the gods became known as Apademak, an indigenous deity of the Kushites. Arkamani I, for the first time in the history of the Kushites, established the right of female monarchs known as Kandake to rule. Although for public ceremonies, these queens had to be accompanied by a male figure. These queens ruled from c. 284 BCE to 314 BCE and the first ever recorded queen was Shanakdakhete in c. 170 BCE. Another queen was Amanirenas from c. 40 BCE to 10 BCE. She led the Kushites into battle during the Meroitic war against Rome, which lasted from 27 BCE to 22 BCE. Rome at that time was under the reign of Augustus Caesar. Queen Amanirenas was able to secure for her people a peace treaty that was favorable.

Economy

The kingdom of Kush, like its ancient Nubian culture, was cosmopolitan. The region has always served as one of the major trading centers connecting the Arabian Desert, Mediterranean basin, and African interior. Nubians imported goods such as timber, incense, bronze, jewelry, stone vessels, wine, olive oil, and clothes from Egypt, the Mediterranean basin, and the Maghreb. The Nubians traded ebony, gold, ivory, hides, ostrich eggs, live animals (such as elephants, giraffes, monkeys, etc.). The Nubian communities were strategic because they opened up to the Red Sea on the east. The Red Sea was a preferred and better avenue for sailing long distances when compared to the Nile. Sometimes, the king of Kush would demand processed goods in exchange for raw materials. The kingdom of Kush played a very important role in the Afro-Eurasian global system where ideas, goods, and even people would be exchanged.

Chapter 3

The land of punt

The Land of Punt, described as "the land of the gods" in ancient Egyptian text, is a region rich in resources. In the year 1822 CE, after Jean-Francois Champollion first deciphered Egyptian hieroglyphics, scholars around the world, after studying the text, began to question as to where the Land of Punt is located today and what could be its modern name. Based on the evidence found from the inscriptions in the deciphered text, it is believed that the Land of Punt is the modern-day Puntland state of Somalia. According to historian Ahmed Abdi, the city of Pouen referenced as part of Punt by ancient inscriptions is identical to the ancient city of Opone in Somalia. The Land of Punt was known as *Pwenet* or *Pwene* to the Egyptians, which is translated as "Pouen." Pouen to the Greek is known as Opone. It is no secret that Opone traded with Egypt many centuries ago.

The Land of Punt is famously known for the expedition of Queen Hatshepsut in 1493 BCE in the Eighteenth Dynasty of Egypt. This brought about the successful first attempt in transplanting foreign fauna as a result of the exchange between Egypt and Punt, which brought back living trees to Egypt. Though this voyage to Punt is famously known, evidence shows that the Egyptians had been trading with the Land of Punt as far back as the Fourth Dynasty (c. 2613–2498 BCE) during Pharaoh Khufu's reign.

Egypt as a nation grew, and in the latter part of the Predynastic period (c. 6000–3150 BCE), trade increased also. The early Dynastic period brought about the firm establishment of trade with Mesopotamia and Phoenician regions. Through trade, Egypt by the Fifth Dynasty (c. 2498–2345) in the Phoenician city of Byblos, and the countries of Punt and Nubia began to flourish. Punt became a major source of cultural and religious influence in as much as it played a major role in trade. It is a land that the Egyptians considered blessed by the gods and a place of their origin.

Location

Among archaeologists, scholars, historians, and others, there exists disputes as to the current location of the Land of Punt. Although over the years, places like present-day Somalia or the Puntland State of Somalia at the Horn of Africa, a part of Arabia, Eritrea, Sudan, or even some regions of East Africa, have been cited to be the exact location of the Land of Punt. Among these places debated by historians and scholars alike, Eritrea and Somalia are the most likely, with Eritrea coming out top since it gained the most acceptance.

However, judging from the expedition of Hatshepsut carved on the temple at Deir al-Bahri, it would seem that the present-day Puntland State of Somalia is the location of the Land of Punt.

Historian Abdisalam Mahamoud is of the view that the ancient Somali name for their region was "Bunn," which is a name referring to the trade with Egypt as "Pwene" or

"Pwenet." This region is known in the present day as "Bunni." From the culture of the Puntland State of Somalia, one can see a similarity in language, ceremonial dress, and arts to that of ancient Egypt.

According to Hatshepsut's inscriptions, it is believed that her mother hailed from Punt. There are also inscriptions pointing Egyptians of the Eighteenth Dynasty to Punt. These Egyptians considered Punt as the source of the origin of their culture. Being intrigued by how proud Hatshepsut was of her expedition to Punt, the scholar John A. Wilson seems to favor Somalia as Punt when he points out the "usual prominence" of this expedition. In his writing, John A. Wilson indicated that it was "the land of incense to the south, perhaps chiefly in the Somaliland area, but also Arabia Felix." There is no way Punt could be in Arabia or Nubia because the Egyptians regularly traded with it, and it was not "to the south"; neither is it the latter since the Egyptians knew that land all too well, and there is nothing "mysterious" about it. Trade conducted via sea travel is also an indication that both Arabia and Nubia are not the Land of Punt. The region of Eritrea seems to be the best contender for Punt since the high possibility that the Land of Punt is located above Somalia and Eritrea fits the bill.

Due to other expeditions and the description of Hatshepsut, some persons favor Somalia as the Land of Punt since the Egyptians traveled there by boat down River Nile, via the Wadi Tumilat in the eastern Delta down to the Red Sea. Evidence also exists that shows the Egyptian crews that visited Punt disassembling their boat and carrying them overland to the Red Sea, hugging the shores as they made their way to Punt. In as much as this description seems to favor an interpretation of Eritrea, the evidence in favor of Somalia is weightier. According to Wilson's pointing to the evidence found at Hatshepsut's temple, the people of the Land of Punt were so thrilled at the arrival of the Egyptians even though it seems like they were living at the edge of the world. Wilson writes:

> The people of Punt are flatteringly amazed at the boldness of the Egyptian sailors: "How did you reach here, the country unknown to men? Did you come down on the ways of heaven, or did you travel by land or sea? How happy God's Land (Punt), which you now tread like Ra!"

Another scholar Marc van de Mieroop, while describing how foreign the Land of Punt was to the Egyptians, writes:

> The Egyptians reached Punt by seagoing boat and found it a country very unlike their own. The representations of houses, animals, and plants suggest a location in northeast Africa along the Red Sea coast, possibly the region of modern Eritrea, although a local farther inland has also been suggested.

Archaeologist Dr. Juris Zarins presented more compelling evidence linking the Land of Punt to Somalia when he argued that during the Neolithic period, settlers from the River Nile valley took over the region of Somalia, and the two years were dominated by trade as early as the second millennium BCE. Dr. Juris Zarins's claim is equally backed up by ancient architectural and cultural evidence strongly linking Punt to Somalia.

Hatshepsut's Expedition to Punt

In as much as trade has been ongoing between the Egyptians and the people of Punt, Hatshepsut's 1493 BCE expedition to Punt holds a special meaning. The reason could be that Hatshepsut's transaction with the Land of Punt was somewhat on a grand scale. However, evidence suggested that Hatshepsut was directed by the gods on how to establish the right connection to Punt after she had lost her way. Based on the reliefs from Hatshepsut temple, the scholar, Wilson, has been able to describe how the voyage was commissioned:

Amun-Ra of Karnak spoke from his sanctum in the temple and directed Hatshepsut to undertake the commercial exploration of the land of Punt. "The majesty of the palace made petition at the stairs of the Lord of the Gods. A command was heard from the Great Throne, an oracle of the god himself, to search out ways to Punt, to explore the roads to the terraces of myrrh."

Making room for the will of the gods, five ships were prepared solely for the journey with lots of goods gathered for trade. Based on the inscriptions from Hatshepsut's reign, Historian Barbara Watterson describes the journey as:

Five ships en route from a port on the Red Sea (possibly Quseir) set out to journey southwards to Suakin, where the expedition disembarked. The voyage had taken between 20 and 25 days, covering on average about 50 kilometers a day, with the ships hugging the coast rather than risk the dangerous deep water of the Red Sea. From Suakin, the route to Punt was overland through the Red Sea hills.

The description of this journey to Punt by land following through the passing of the Red Sea could be a major contender for Eritrea or Somalia as long as the other pieces of evidence are taken into consideration. The houses at Punt are set on stilts, and the people of Punt are governed by a king who had elders as his advisers. According to inscriptions, the people of Punt were described as being extremely generous, and the relations between Punt and Egypt were very good. Egyptian scribes have never been shy of their praise for the Land of Punt, for its riches and "goodness."

Egypt, Punt, and Trade

A relief from the Fourth Dynasty has shown one of Pharaoh Khufu's sons with a Puntite, and documents from the Fifth Dynasty have shown both countries enriching themselves through regular trade. An inscription from military commander Pepynakht Heqalb, who served under King Pepy II (2278–2184 BCE) of the Sixth Dynasty, told of how he was sent by King Pepy II to "the Land of Aamu" to retrieve the body of Kekhen, the warden who was killed by the Aamu and the Sand-dwellers when he was building a reed boat from the Land of Aamu to travel to Punt. The Sand-dwellers were from Sudan, while the Aamu were Asiatics of Arabia contending for the port of Suakin (as earlier noted by Watterson) for a departure point for Egyptian trade on the west coast of the Red Sea. The trade with Punt was needed by the Egyptians for many of Punt's prized possessions.

Ebony, gold, wild animals, elephant tusks, ivory, spices, precious woods, animal skins, cosmetics, incense, myrrh trees, and frankincense were the items brought to Egypt from Punt. Historian Barbara Watterson writes: "In return for a modest present of a few Egyptian weapons and some trinkets, the Puntites gave their visitors sacks of aromatic gum, gold, ebony, ivory, leopard skins, live apes, and incense trees." From Watterson's description, it might seem that the trade between both countries was one-sided, but with the inscription, we saw a fair-trade exchange between both countries. Wilson, while reporting how the Egyptians arrived at Punt, writes with "jewelry, tools, and weapons" and returned with "incense trees, ivory, myrrh, and rare woods." Evidence also suggests that Egyptians, having their own gold mines traded metals from their country for Punt's gold.

As stated earlier, the fauna (plants and trees), being an impressive article of trade, was successfully transplanted in another country during Egyptian trade with Punt. The fauna, being the first time in history its transplant had happened in another soil, was not only successful, it even flourished for centuries in Egypt. Outside the Hatshepsut complex at Deir al-Bahri, the root of the Frankincense tree brought from her expedition to Punt in 1493 BCE can still be seen. According to the inscriptions found on the wall of the site, Egyptians and the people of Punt held each other in deep respect, and the trade between both countries was mutually beneficial. Also, there exists evidence from the temple that shows the envoys from Egypt being received with honor by the Puntite chief and his wife. So vivid was the description that scholars and historians have been able to diagnose the Puntite wife of Chief Aty's medical challenges. Historian Jimmy Dunn writes that the queen "shows signs of lipodystrophy or Dercum's disease. She had a pronounced curvature of the spinal column." A segment of the inscriptions referenced Perehu, who was a king of Punt at that time, and his generosity, which was seen in the vast goods brought back to Egypt. In as much as the reign of Queen Hatshepsut was one of the most prosperous in the history of Egypt, nothing trumps her expedition to Punt. Watterson, explaining the inscriptions found at the queen's temple at Deir al-Bahri, writes of how important Punt was to the queen: "Reliefs depicting important themes from Hatshepsut's life decorate walls in the colonnades: her birth, the transportation of obelisks for the Temple of Amun in Thebes, the great expedition to Punt."

Marc van de Mieroop also lends his own voice to this comment by saying: "Complete incense trees as well as loose incense, an expensive fragrant tree extract that was used in religious services as an offering to the gods" were among the goods imported. The expedition gathered a large amount of it (incense), and the accompanying inscription describes how those quantities were never acquired before. How prominent the relief was, shows the pride that Hatshepsut awarded the achievements of her expedition.

In addition to the valuable things mentioned above, thirty-one incense trees (Boswellia) were also brought back to Egypt from Punt, which made the visit of Punt as important as the goods traded there.

Egypt's legendary past and gods have a strong affiliation with the Land of Punt since some of the materials used in the Egyptian temple for rituals were obtained from Punt. For instance, the leopard skin worn by the priest, the gold used in the sanctuary, and the incense burned in the temple were from Punt. It is believed that the gods that shower the Land of Egypt with their goodness had like affection for the Land of Punt. Evidence suggests that the dwarf-god, known as the "god of childbirth," was equally from Punt. The same is said of other gods of Egypt (with Hatshepsut's mother, Hathor not excluded), all having Punt as their origin.

Legend of Punt and the Modern Day

Punt became immortalized in the Egyptian literature during the Twelfth Dynasty (1991–1802 BCE) as the popular tale of a castaway Egyptian sailor who was shipwrecked on an island, finding himself conversing with a serpent that calls itself the "Lord of Punt." The great serpent aided the Egyptian sailor in locating his way back to Egypt, laden with spices, gold, and unique animals. The sailor, on arriving home, tells his master of his encounter with the great serpent in order to encourage him after a failed expedition, knowing how disappointed his master must feel since he himself had encountered worse – fearing for his life and losing his ship also.

Since the Land of Punt had been linked with the gods in the past, it was intentionally chosen in this tale as the mystical island the sailor was washed up upon. The sailor's message to his master was simple, and it is that even in the darkest moment of one's life, when life looks bleak, and it seems like all hope is lost, good can still happen. This, the sailor did by reminding his master and anyone who would later hear of the tale of the gods and their blessings by pointing to the fact that his voyage that was doomed for failure ended up enriching him with the "Lord of Punt" turning his fortunes around.

Through the New Kingdom (1570–1069 BCE), the Land of Punt that until then was a semi-mythical land to the Egyptians became a very real place. Tributes from foreign delegates to the Land of Punt were accepted by the Vizier, Rekhmira, in the reign of Amunhotep II (1425–1400 BCE). Punt was equally mentioned during the reign of Ramesses II the Great (1279–1213 BCE) and Ramesses III (1186–1155 BCE). The Egyptians became so fascinated with the Land of Punt and have come to know her as a "Land of Plenty," calling Punt Te Netjer, the land of the gods, from which every good thing comes to Egypt. Punt, on the other hand, came to see the Land of Egypt as their ancient homeland, having associated with Egyptian ancestry, calling it the land where the gods emerged from and consorted with each other. The Land of Punt that was so exalted from reality into mythology came to a decline in the minds of Egyptians after the reign of Ramesses III until it was lost both in legend and folklore.

Today, the people of Somalia still keep the customs and language of ancient Egypt alive as a way of honoring their relationship with the people of Egypt. Citing English linguist Charles Barber, historian Abdislam Mahamoud describes how the language of ancient Egypt came from the Hamitic group of languages still spoken "across a large part of North Africa including Somali." Mahamoud, referencing this citing, commented on how people in modern-day Somalia continue naming their children after ancient Egyptian gods – for instance, being called in modern-day language "Oraxthy" from the ancient Egyptian "Horakhty." Even though the Land of Punt may have slowly disappeared into mythology in ancient Egypt, its rich heritage is still being preserved by those in the present day who choose to remember their past and honor it.

Chapter 4

Carthage

The Carthage city founded on the coast of northwest Africa in the 9th century BCE is located in present-day Tunisia, being one of the Phoenician settlements in the Western Mediterranean, created for the purpose of facilitating trade from the city of Tyre, Sidon, and others on the coast of present-day Lebanon. Throughout the Mediterranean, Carthage developed into a major trading empire with both its name and city coming into the limelight. Though there is no significant data attesting to when Carthage became an independent power, neither is there anything that can distinguish Carthage from other colonies in the Northwest region of Africa and the Mediterranean during 800–700 BCE. Carthage's commercial value shot to the limelight at the end of the 7th century BCE when it was fast becoming the leading commercial center of the West Mediterranean region. After the Punic Wars (the long conflict with the emerging Roman Republic in 264–146 BCE), Carthage was finally destroyed by Rome in 146 BCE, with its water supply cut off, its walls torn down, and its harbor rendered unusable following its defeat at the hand of the Arab invaders at the end of 7th century. Tunis later became the major regional center that replaced Carthage and has expanded to include the ancient site of Carthage as a modern suburb.

Originally, Carthage was known as Kart-hadasht (new city) in order to distinguish it from the older Phoenician city of Utica nearby. While the Greeks call it Karchedon, the Romans turned this name into Carthage. It was founded by the Legendary Queen Dido in 814 BCE, and it expanded following the conquest of Alexander the Great (332 BCE) with the immigration of refugees from the city of Tyre. It continued expanding until it became the seat of the Carthaginian Empire with colonies (such as Sabratha) along the North Africa regions, in Sicily and Spain. These were lost as a result of the Punic Wars, which saw Rome take Carthage's former position as the greatest Mediterranean power.

Into five periods was the history of the ancient city of Carthage divided. They are Ancient Carthage (Punic Republic) in 814–146 BCE, Roman Carthage in 146 BCE to 439 CE, Vandal Carthage in 439–534 CE, Byzantine Carthage (Exarchate of Africa) in 534–698 CE, and the Muslim Arab Carthage (Islamic Carthage) in 698–1270 CE.

The ancient city of Carthage was conquered and destroyed in the period 698 BCE during the Arab Muslim invasion of North Africa. In as much as it was later rebuilt, though, to a moderate scale, it was finally destroyed under Muhammad I al-Mustansir's reign (r. 1228–1277 CE), after conquering the European Christian invasion of the Eighth Crusade of 1270 CE. Though still inhabited, its ancient ruins were left that way until when modern excavations began in the 1830s CE.

Foundation and Expansion

Legend has it that the Phoenician Queen Elissa (better known as Dido) founded Carthage in c. 814 BCE. Dido, while running away from the tyranny of her brother Pygmalion of Lebanon, found herself in the region of North Africa. There, she established the city on the high hill that was later known as Byrsa. The legend further lets us know that the Berber chieftain, who was the overseer of that region, told Dido that she could have as many lands as an ox hide can take. So, Dido got an ox hide and cut them into smaller pieces laying them end to end to claim the island for herself and her people.

According to the Roman poet Virgil (l. 70–19 BCE) and other accounts, Dido's reign was described as impressive, taking into consideration how the city that was a small community on the hill grew into a gigantic metropolis. This was so legendary that Carthage, which seems to be a minor spot where the Phoenician traders would stop to either repair their ship or restock their supply, became a major trade center in the 4th century BCE.

In 332 BCE, the city developed significantly following Alexander's destruction of the great industrial and trade center of Tyre (known as Carthage's mother-city) with Phoenician refugees fleeing to Carthage with all manner of wealth they had left since Alexander only spared those of rich means. These men coming to Carthage with their wealth only enforced the city as the new center of Phoenician trade.

Not wasting any time, the Carthaginians quickly established a working relationship with the Masaesyli tribes and the Massylii of the North Africa Berber (Imazighen) Kingdom of Numidia, who would occupy the ranks of their military, forming a formidable cavalry. From a small town on a hill, Carthage soon became the richest and most powerful city in the Mediterranean with large estates covering large acreage of lands.

By the 4th century BCE, Carthage's government, which was formerly a monarchy, became a republic-based meritocracy (a system where the elite of the society rules) with two elected magistrates known as Suffetes ("judges") occupying the top position. The Suffetes were to govern alongside a senate of between two hundred to three hundred members who would occupy that position for life. The assembly of citizens would vote on the measures put forward by the Suffetes and senate; only then would the law be passed. The lowest in the society lived in huts or apartments outside the city. The middle-class lived in beautiful and attractive homes while the aristocrats had their dwellings in the palace.

Apart from the major lucrative business in maritime trade, money also came in through tariffs and tributes. These also helped in boosting the economy of Carthage. The city harbor was properly immense, having a gleaming column in a half-circle around it with capacity for 220 ships. In front of it were towering arches and buildings designed with Greek sculptures. The two harbors that existed in the city were for trade and resupplying, repairing and outfitting warship vessels. Around the Mediterranean Sea, the Carthaginian trading ships sailed daily to ports, with their navy ensuring their people were safe by keeping guard of the water and also conquering new territories for trade and resources, which in turn extended Carthage boundaries all the more.

Carthage had four residential sections, which were around Byrsa acting as a stronghold at the center, surrounded by walls stretching twenty-three miles in length from the inland of the harbor. Just like any great city, Carthage had a theater for entertainment, a temple for religious activities, a necropolis, a marketplace that was very grand, beautiful accommodation structures and refinements. The goddess of love and fertility, Tanit, alongside her consort Baal-Hamon were the patron deities of Carthage. Though this claim has been challenged, it was purported that children were sacrificed to Tanit in the sacred precinct of Tophet. It is possible that the Tophet of Carthage city was simply a necropolis kept for infants and the young.

Affluence and Invasion

The wealth of Carthage was not only because of how well they were positioned on the North Africa coast, which put them in a very advantageous position in controlling traffic at sea between the city and Sicily. The wealth of Carthage can also be pointed to its people's skills in agriculture. The author of Mago of Carthage wrote a comprehensive twenty-eight volume book that was devoted to the science of agriculture and veterinarian study, which simply reflects the intense interest of the Carthaginians in farming and animal husbandry at the time. Mago's work was so significant that they were among the few spared by the Romans in 146 BCE after the final defeat of Carthage. Now all that remains from that work are just a few references from the Romans.

The Carthaginians planted vegetables, olive trees, grapes, and fruit trees and then expanded cultivation all the way to the field of grains. Carthage continued to flourish as the city's wealth through trade with the interior as well as maritime trade elsewhere increased through their expertise in cultivation and the fertility of the land.

The first conflict the city of Carthage ever experienced with others was as a result of their expansion. North Africa was invaded in 310–307 BCE by Agathocles of Syracuse (r. 317–289 BCE), who sought Carthage wealth for war. Though Agathocles was able to feed his men from the rich crops that grew in abundance on the land, he was defeated because the Libyans and Berbers who worked the land were on the side of the Carthaginians since the Carthaginians were agreeable to them. So, Agathocles and his men were driven from North Africa. In 264 BCE, Carthage became involved in a conflict with Rome, which was a small city-state on the Tiber River in Italy.

The Punic Wars

The conflict with Rome began over the control of Sicily since it was now divided between Rome and Carthage and their support for the opposing factions on the island quickly brought both parties against each other. This conflict is what later led to what we call the Punic Wars today. When compared to Carthage, Rome posed no threat as it was weak and the Carthaginian navy in the past had successfully been able to keep the Romans from trading west of the Mediterranean.

To Carthaginians' surprise, Rome proved to have far more resources than Carthage could imagine when the First Punic War began in 264–241 BCE. Rome, with no navy and no idea of fighting on the sea, quickly built 330 ships, equipping them with gangways and ingenious ramps that could be lowered into an enemy ship to secure it. After a series of military tactics, Rome came out on top, causing Carthage to cede Sicily and thereby pay a heavy price. Carthage was defeated by Rome in 241 BCE.

In 241–237 BCE, immediately after the war, Carthage became drawn into what is known as the Mercenary War. This was when the Carthaginian mercenaries were demanding that the debt owed to them be paid. Carthage won the Mercenary War with the help of general Hamilcar Barca (I. c. 285–c. 228 BCE).

Carthage suffered greatly in the aftermath of the First Punic and the Mercenary War, and even when Rome occupied Carthaginian colonies of Sardinia and Corsica, there was nothing the Carthaginians could do about it. Making the best of what they now had seemed to be the best idea. This Carthage did, which led them to go to war again with Rome when they tried to expand their holdings in Spain by attacking an ally of Rome known as the city of Saguntum in 218 BCE. The attack was led by Hannibal.

In 218–202 BCE, the Second Punic War was fought in Northern Italy. Hannibal marching his troops into the Alps, invaded Italy from Spain, and he won every engagement with the Romans in Italy. In 216 BCE, Hannibal came out victorious at the Battle of Cannae but, due to insufficient supplies and troops, he could not build on his successes. He was finally drawn from Italy at the battle of Zama in North Africa in 202 BCE and was defeated by the Roman general Scipio Africanus (l. 236–183 BCE). This led to Carthage suing for peace again and Rome placing Carthage again under a heavy war indemnity. Carthage, not enjoying the spoils of war, was battling to pay off their debt while also trying to fend off an attack from their neighbors, Numidia, an ally of Rome during the Second Punic War under King Masinissa (r. c. 202–148 BCE). Numidia was encouraged by Rome to raid the Carthaginians at will. As such, the Carthaginians went to war against King Masinissa of Numidia, and in so doing, broke the peace treaty they had with the Romans. The peace treaty stated that the Carthaginians were forbidden to mobilize an army, and that was what they did against Numidia. According to Rome's sanction, Carthage now had to pay a war debt to Numidia after they just came out of one with Rome. Even though Carthage felt that they had no choice but to defend themselves against Numidia, Rome wasn't concerned, neither were they pleased with Carthage for revitalizing their military.

Carthage thinking that their treaty with Rome ended when they paid off their debt was greatly mistaken as Rome did not see it as so. The Romans still wanted to bend Carthage to do their bidding that the Roman senator Cato Elder in all his speeches, no matter the subject, always ended with the phrase "Further, I think Carthage must be destroyed." In 149 BCE, Rome decided upon that course of action, and Carthage was destroyed.

The Roman embassy to Carthage stipulated that Carthage be dismantled completely and then rebuilt further inland, all in an attempt to render its once-held position and long-standing advantage over trade on the coast unrecognizable. To this effect, the Carthaginians refused, and this led to the Third Punic War in 149–146 BCE.

For three years, the Roman general, Scipio Aemilianus (l. 185–129 BCE) besieged Carthage until it fell. After ransacking it, the Romans burned the city to the ground leaving no stone unturned. According to the report, after ordering the destruction of the city, Scipio Aemilianus wept and behaved virtuously toward the survivors of the siege.

While Carthage lay in ruins, Utica now became the capital of Rome's African province. In 122 BCE, Gaius Sempronius Gracchus (l. 154–121 BCE), the Roman tribune, founded a small colony where Carthage used to be. This colony did not last because of Gaius's political problems and the fact that the memory of the Punic Wars still lingered. Carthage rose again five years after the death of Julius Caesar, who planned to have it rebuilt in the first instance. Soon power shifted to Carthage from Utica since it was now the breadbasket of the Romans, owing to the agricultural fields that were still productive. Under the Romans, Carthage became a very important colony until 439 CE where it fell to the Vandals under King Gaiseric (r. 428–478 CE).

Later on, Carthage rose to prominence as Christianity grew. St. Augustine of Hippo (l. 354–430 CE) contributed to its prestige by living out life and teaching there. The Council of Carthage was held at the city because of its illustrious nature, and the Bible was as a result of the Council meeting on so many occasions so as to come up with a generally accepted and established way of life for the Western Church.

The invasion of the North by Vandals did not stop the Christianity movement there, just as the tension between the Arian Christians and Trinitarian Christians exists everywhere else.

The vandals taking advantage of their new location under the leadership of Gaiseric, plundered passing ships at will; the Romans attempted to displace them but failed, so a treaty was signed between Gaiseric and Valentinian III (r. 425–455 CE) in 442 CE. The treaty acknowledged the Vandal kingdom as a true political entity, thereby establishing peaceful relations. In 455 CE, Valentinian III was assassinated; Gaiseric disregarded the peace treaty on the account that it was between the emperor and himself. So, he set sail to Rome. He looted the city but didn't damage it or touch the populace. This was in accordance with the request from Pope Leo I

(440–461). Until the death of Gaiseric, Vandals continued to profit from Carthage.

The persecution of Trinitarian Christians was reinstituted by the later Vandal King Gelimer (r. 530–534), who was an Arian Christian. His actions on the Trinitarian Christians enraged the trinitarian Roman Emperor from the East, Emperor Justinian I (r. 527–565 CE), who deployed his best general Belisarius (l. 505–565 CE) to North Africa. Belisarius, in the Vandalic War of 553–534 CE, won against Gelimer, bringing him back in chains to Constantinople, thereby restoring Carthage to the Byzantine Empire (330–1453 CE) from which she flourished.

Carthage prospered through trade under the Byzantines, providing the majority of grains for the Eastern Roman Empire. In around, 585 CE, under the Byzantine Emperor, Maurice (r. 582–602 CE), the Exarchate of Africa became Carthage. This administrative region was established separately for a more effective ruling of the Western areas of the empire.

In 698 CE, at the battle of Carthage, the Muslims defeated the Byzantine forces, driving them completely out of Africa and fully destroying the city. Subsequently, the neighboring city Tunis was fortified and developed, which became the new trade and governorship center for the region. Under the reign of the Arab Muslims, Tunis fared better than Carthage still, Carthage kept thriving until 1270 CE. This period ushered in the Eight Crusade, that is, European Crusaders took over and fortified the citadel of Byrsa. Once they were conquered, Muhammad I al-Mustansir gave the order for the city's defense to be brought down, including many of the buildings razed to the ground to prevent any further habitation.

Legacy

The conflict with the Romans is how best the world remembers Carthage, especially the Second Punic War – an event that may likely have changed the course of human history, seeing the roles the Romans played in Christianity, European history, and Western Civilization. Greek and Roman observers are often intrigued at Carthage and at the height of its power before the First Punic War, and they often pay tribute to Carthage's wealth, prosperity, and sophisticated republican governmental structure. The Punic Wars and the years following its destructions have led many to have a rethink of Carthage and all its wonders, with so many accounts of its civilization reflecting biases with propaganda shaped as a result of its numerous crises. Carthage, often portrayed for its political, cultural, and military prowess, fell to Rome, a place where "cruelty, treachery and irreligion" reigned. Now we are left with a slanted depiction of Carthage for centuries as a result of the dominant influence of the Greco-Roman perspectives in Western history.

The 20th century ushered in a more critical and well-detailed record backed by archaeological evidence across the Mediterranean, showing the civilization of Carthage to be more complex than we even anticipated. With its vast and lucrative commercial network touching every part of the ancient world, from the British Isles to Western and Central Africa and beyond, Carthaginians were enterprising and pragmatic, just like their Phoenician ancestors. They demonstrated a remarkable capacity to adapt and be innovative even when the circumstances changed, like the existential threat encountered during the Punic Wars. While art and literature might not do Carthage any justice, there exists circumstantial evidence pointing to its multicultural and sophisticated civilization connecting people across ancient worlds, mixing their ideas, cultures, society into its own framework.

Portrayal in Fiction

Gustave Flaubert's historical novel *Salammbô* (1862) speaks of Carthage set around the time of the Mercenary War. It speaks of the boy Hannibal escaping being sacrificed; it describes in dramatic fashion child sacrifice. The film *Cabiria* by Giovanni Pastrone is narrowly based on Flaubert's novel.

The science fiction short story by Isaac Asimov called "The Dead Past," in which the main character is a historian of antiquity, is disapproving of the claims that Carthaginians carried out child sacrifices.

The boy's adventure novel by G. A. Henty titled *The Young Carthaginian* (1887) is told from Malchus's perspective about a teenage lieutenant of Hannibal during the Second Punic War.

The *Purple Quest* by Frank G. Slaughter is a fictional description of how Carthage was founded.

The Dying City is another fictional work of art that tells the story of the city of Carthage, such as the battle with the Romans and the defeat of Hannibal that came at the hand of Scipio Africanus at the great battle of Zama, written by Antonie P. Roux in Afrikaans and published in 1956.

Alternate History

The short story in Poul Anderson's *Time Patrol* series, "Delenda Est," depicts an alternate history where Hannibal won the Second Punic War, and Carthage still existed in the 20th century.

Stephen Baxter, featuring Carthage in his alternate history, *Northland* trilogy, tells of how Carthage prevails over and subjugates Rome.

John Maddox Roberts's two-part fiction, which includes *Hannibal's Children* (2002) and *The Seven Hills* (2005), is set in an alternate history where the defeat of Rome in the Second Punic War came through the hand of Hannibal and Carthage is still a major Mediterranean force to reckon with in 100 BCE.

Government

As earlier stated, the Carthaginian government was divided into a monarchy consisting of the Shophet, which was the king and the council of one hundred and four, known as the senate. Both the Shophet and the senate had the support of some segment of the population. The Shophets, for instance, had the allegiance of the military and the priests while the senate commanded the support of the merchants and that of the common people in its society. Both the Shophet and the senate were constantly after power. It was all about who held the greatest power in the kingdom, and this can be seen in the kingdom's history. At times, the king wielded more power, especially before the conflict with the Romans. But when Carthage began to lose to the Romans, political power then shifted to the hands of the council. The following list shows the Shophets according to their dynasty.

Didonids

The Didonian line consists of Dido and her direct descendants, who were of the semi-legendary founder of Carthage. Carthage prospered under their rule as a city of exploration and trade. The following are the Didonians;

Dido – 814–760 B.C.

Hanno I – 580–556 B.C.

Malchus – 556–550 B.C.

Magonids

The Magonids are of general Mago I descent, who overthrew Malchus because of his incompetence and married his (Malchus's) daughter afterward so as to draw legitimacy from the Didonian line. Carthage became a major military and colonial powerhouse under the Magonids. However, there was a fluctuation in power depending on the Shophet in power and his opposition. The Magonids include:

Mago I – 550–530 B.C.

Hasdrubal I – 530–510 B.C.

Hamilcar I – 510–480 B.C.

Hanno II – 480–440 B.C.

Himilco I – 440–406 B.C.

Mago II – 406–396 B.C.

Himlico II – 396–375 B.C.

Mago III – 375–344 B.C.

Hanno III – 344–340 B.C

Bomilcarids

Senator Bomilcar using marriage and assassination, rose to power and won himself the throne. Under the Bomilcarids' short stint in power, the island of Sicily was conquered by the

Greeks and finally lost to the Romans. The Bomilcarids include:

Bomilcar – 340–312 B.C.

Hasdrubal I – 312–274 B.C.

Gisco I – 274–240 B.C.

Barcids

The city of Carthage became orderly when Barcids came into power, unlike in the time of Bomilcarids' reign. Barcids set out to reform the economic and military structure of the land. It was during his reign that Carthage almost defeated the Romans though they ended up losing to the Romans. The Barcids include:

Hamilcar II – 240–228 B.C.

Hannibal – 228–179 B.C.

Hasdrubal II – 179–162 B.C.

Gisco II – 162–157 B.C.

Economy

At its height, the Carthaginian economy dominated the Mediterranean, even stretching across Africa to the point of maintaining many of the ancient trade routes and landmarks of its Phoenician ancestors who had also used that route during their days. Precious silks and the raw materials required to produce purple dye, which are valuable murex shells, were accessible to the Carthaginians. Carthage still retained much of its Phoenician economic legacy. Carthage also traded fish, various textiles, gold, silver, copper, tin, iron, lead, ivory, glass, wood, and other products.

Northern Africa and Hispania were the major suppliers of Carthage resources. The economy shifted as Carthage begin to lose ground to the rising Romans from solely based on trade to agriculture. During this phase, crops were used for growing the Mediterranean, with wine and grains becoming the largest agricultural export across the Mediterranean.

Agriculture

North Africa hinterland is known to be fertile, having the ability to support the growing of crops and the rearing of livestock. According to Diodorus in the 4th century BCE sharing an eyewitness account, the gardens were beautiful, with a green plantation, the estates were luxurious and large with a vast network of artificial water supply systems to give water to the land. In the mid-second century BCE, the visiting Roman envoys including Cato the Censor described Carthage's countryside as a place where humans and animals flourish. Cato the Censor is known for his low regard as far as foreign culture is concerned, as well as his fondness for agriculture. Writing of his own experience when he visited at the same period, Polybius is of the opinion that there seemed to be a high production of livestock in Carthage as compared to other cities of the world.

Just like their Phoenician ancestors, Carthaginians didn't originally engage in agriculture. Many of the Phoenician colonies were like Carthage, located primarily along the coast, but as they settled more inland, the Carthaginians eventually took advantage of the region's rich soil developing what may have been one of the most diversified and prosperous agricultural sectors of all time – using iron ploughs, irrigation, crop rotation, threshing machines, hand-driven rotary mills, and horse mills, Carthaginians practiced productive and advanced agriculture.

Even in the face of adversity, Carthage was looking for ways to refine their agricultural techniques. Hannibal promoted agriculture after the Second Punic War to help restore Carthage's economy and to pay off the heavy war indemnity levelled on them by the Romans. The money levied on Carthage was about 10,000 talents, which equals 800,000 pounds of Roman silver, and Hannibal was very successful in paying it via agriculture. Strabo, while reporting of the years leading to the Third Punic War, noted how the devasted and improvised Carthage had made its land flourish again through agriculture. To fully understand the weight of agriculture to the Carthaginians, consider two of the retired generals known to modern-day history, Hamilcar and Mago, who made agriculture and agronomy a major part of their reign. Mago was so successful in agriculture that he had to put his knowledge in books totaling twenty-eight volumes.

These are the few materials the Romans refuse to destroy; instead, it was translated into Latin because of its rich content. Though the original copies might be lost to history, references to it from Greek and Roman writers still remain.

Circumstantial evidence pointed to the fact that before the 4th century BCE, Carthage developed viticulture and wine production. The wine produced was exported as a cigar-shaped amphora and was found in one of the archaeological sites attesting to Carthage wine production and exports.

Carthage also shipped resin wine, also known as *passum* in Latin, popular in antiquity even among the Romans. Figs, pears, and pomegranates known as "Punic apples" to the Romans were cultivated in the hinterland while olive oil was exported across the Mediterranean. Carthage also bred fine horses, which were the ancestors of today's Barb horses used for racing today and considered most influential breed after the Arabian.

Conclusion

The site that once housed the ancient city continued to be inhabited and was included as part of the Ottoman Empire in 1299–1922 CE, which was unwilling to excavate its ruins. The materials of the fallen houses, temples, and even the walls were either used for personal or administrative projects or were left where they had been found. In the 1830s CE, modern excavation began through the efforts of the Danish consulate and continued under the French between c. 1860–1900 CE.

Though further work was undertaken at the site in the first half of the 20th century, archaeologists showed more interest in the Roman history of Carthage at Sabratha and other sites. According to the cultural and political zeitgeist of that time, the Carthaginians who were Semites were defined as a people of little value, and the anti-Semitism influenced the physical evidence as well as the choice of what was kept for placement in museums or discarded.

The history of ancient Carthage still suffers not just from the city's destruction by Rome or later conflicts but from modern-day excavations also. World War II ushered in an unbiased, systematic work of ancient Carthage that serves as a template for viewing and interpreting many of the other ancient sites found. In modern-day Tunisia, Carthage still lies in ruins, which remains an important tourist and archaeological site to this day. The ruins of homes and the outlines of the great harbor can still be seen, including public baths, temples, palaces from the time when the city was the wonder of the Mediterranean as well as the jewel of the North African coast.

Chapter 5

Kingdom of aksum

The Kingdom of Aksum is also called the Aksumite Empire or even sometimes, the Kingdom of Axum; it was a kingdom that had territory spanning the northern part of Ethiopia, specifically in the region known as Tigray and also the area that is currently known as Eritrea. Men who have ruled the Kingdom of Aksum usually branded themselves with titles such as king of kings, King of Aksum, Himyar, Raydan, Salhen, Saba, Tsiyamo, and Beja of Kush. The kingdom stood for many decades, being in existence from 80 BCE to 825 CE. The kingdom's capital, where its ruler lived and exercised his administrative authority as well as discharged his duties, was located in Aksum city, and it started growing in the earliest (Iron Age) era of the kingdom's existence – particularly around the 4th century BCE and around the 1st century CE, the kingdom became well known. Sometime in history, the kingdom of Aksum grew to the point where it played a major role in the trade existing between the Empire of Rome and ancient India.

In order to make trade possible, the monarchs of the Kingdom of Aksum started to print their own money as well as laying the groundwork for their form of government, especially as the Kingdom of Kush was gradually waning at the time. From time to time, the Kingdom of Aksum started to interfere with the political issues of other kingdoms, especially those on the Arabian Peninsula, to the point that its power and authority spread vastly over that area when it conquered the Himyarite Kingdom. As at CE 274, a prophet of Manichaei known as Mani stated that Aksum was one of the greatest powers of that time alongside Rome, Persia, and China. Aksum ruled over South Arabia of Yemen for about fifty years in the 6th century.

For the purpose of religion, the people of the Kingdom of Aksum crafted monumental stelae, which they worshipped before the coming of Christianity. One of the stelae crafted by its people is today, the largest such structure in the world at ninety feet tall. It was during the reign of Ezana (fl. 320–360) that Christianity became adopted by Aksumites.

The ancient capital of the Kingdom of Aksum is also known as Aksum, and it is now a town in the Tigray Region (Northern Ethiopia). The kingdom took on the name "Ethiopia" in the 4th century. It is said that the kingdom is the place where the Ark of the Covenant was rested; further claims of their tradition also states that it was the home of the Queen of Sheba.

History

There are many theories that have been propounded about the history of Ethiopia and most of them by Carlo Conti Rossini; it was his theories that led many to believe that it was the Sabaeans whose spoken language was taken out of a Semitic branch of the major Afro-Asiatic language family that established the Kingdom of Aksum. Despite this fact, there is proof that there were Aksumites who already spoke the Semitic language, and it was these people who also adopted the Agaw people that were already speaking a different Afro-Asiatic language from the Cushitic branch of the family; furthermore, the Semitic Aksumites had already created an autonomous civilization in the Ethiopian territory before even the Sabaeans arrived.

Furthermore, more scholars discovered evidence that in such kingdoms as D'mt, there were growth and prosperity around the 10th and 15th centuries BCE, long before the Sabaeans migrated to the area in the 4th or 5th century BCE. In addition, evidence points out that the Sabaeans who settled in the area did not stay for a long time, leaving after a couple of years. All these points have thus greatly reduced the connotation that the Sabeans had anything to do with the happenings in the era at the time. Only very few settlements believe that the Sabaeans did anything in their areas, such as making up the trade group or military of one colony or another – particularly having military alliances with the D'mt civilization or an ancient state in Aksum. In the words of a scholar known as George Hatke:

> The most significant and lasting impact of these colonists was the establishment of a writing system and the introduction of Semitic speech – both of which the Ethiopians modified considerably. South Arabian culture was a foreign commodity from which the Ethiopians were able to freely pick and choose when they saw fit, rather than an entire civilization imposed by foreign rulers.
>
> The Ge'ez language is no longer universally thought of, as previously assumed, to be an offshoot of Sabaean or Old South Arabian, and there is some

linguistic (though not written) evidence of Semitic languages being spoken in Eritrea and Ethiopia since approximately 2000 BCE. However, the Ge'ez script later replaced Epigraphic South Arabian in the Kingdom of Aksum.

The language, Ge'ez, is not considered as derived from Sabaean or Old South Arabian any longer, unlike in previous times when it was. In fact, scholars have found proof of a spoken language in Eritrea and Ethiopia as of 2000 BCE, although the language was not written.

Empire

Aksum was a kingdom that was deeply invested in trade, and the location of the trading centers were first in Eritrea, and second, the northern part of Ethiopia. It was a kingdom that was in existence around 100–940 CE; the kingdom stemmed from the Iron Age – which was the early Aksum period – the 4th century BCE right to the year it became well-known in the 1st century CE. The first capital of the kingdom known as Mazaber was built by the son of Cush whose name was Itiyopis. Sometime later, the capital of the kingdom was moved to Axum in northern Ethiopia. The name Ethiopia was later adopted by the empire in the 4th century.

The entire territory that was owned by the Kingdom of Aksum covered the whole of contemporary Eritrea, Ethiopia, Somalia, Djibouti, and Yemen, and some areas in Sudan. The capital city that is also called by the same name, Aksum, is currently located in northern Ethiopia; however, as years have passed, the city is nothing more than a small community. Although in times past, the city was a place where all kinds of cultural and economic events were held, and it was filled with a lot of energy. There were two hills to the east side of the city, while to the west there were two streams; it is usually thought that these were the reasons why people became interested in settling in the city initially. Toward the hills and plains lying outside of the city, there are cemeteries that belong to people of Aksum and in these cemeteries are gravestones that are very detailed, and they are called stelae, or obelisks. Other major cities in the empire include Yeba, Hawulti-Melazo, Matara, Adulis, and Qohaito – among these mentioned cities, the latter three are at present in Eritrea. At the time when Endubis exercised rulership over the empire in the latter part of the 3rd century, the empire had started coining its own money; the currency was named by Mani, who said that the empire was one of the four great powers of the world at the time while the others include the Sasanian Empire, Roman Empire and "Three Kingdoms" China. Around 325 or 328 CE, the Kingdom of Aksum had adopted Christianity as the religion of the kingdom. The ruler in power at the time was King Ezana; the empire was the first to start using the picture of the cross on its coins.

Within the 3rd century, probably between c. 240, and c. 260, the people of Aksum were led to victory over the people of Sesea by *Sembrouthes*, and afterward, Sesea became a tributary of the Aksum Empire. In c. 330, King Ezana of the Kingdom of Aksum led his army into war against the Kingdom of Meroē and claimed the kingdom for himself after he conquered it. Afterward, a monument made of stone was left there, and this story is also related to Ezana Stone.

Decline

In the early 6th century, there was a second golden age, and this was followed by the waning of the Aksum Empire, which happened precisely in the middle of the 6th century, and this came to a point where the kingdom stopped minting its own coins during the early part of the 7th century. It was still during this period that the people of Aksum started to desert the capital city in a bid to go deep into the highlands believing that they would be protected there. During this time, Arab scholars still depicted Ethiopia (it was no longer called Aksum) as a state that had a vast land and was indeed powerful, even though the state no longer had control over the coasts and tributaries that were once under it. Be that as it may, whenever they lost land in the north, they found a way to gain land in the south; furthermore, Ethiopia was not a great economic power. Regardless, Arab merchants were still drawn to the state. The capital of the state was then moved; the current location is unknown, nevertheless, it was called Ku'bar or Jami.

A couple of years later, the Red Sea and Egypt were taken over in the year 646 by the Rashidun Caliphate, and this made the Aksum Empire fall into a state of isolation economically. To the northwest of Aksum, which is currently the country known as Sudan, Christian states such as Nobatia, Makuria, and Alodia survived for a long time, even until the 13th century before they converted to Islam. Although, despite being in an isolated state, the people of Aksum remained Christians.

While Degna Dian was exercising rulership over the Aksum Empire in the 10th century, Aksum continued to take over territory toward the south and even sent its army into the region that is now known as Kaffa; and at the same time, it was carrying out missionary duties in Amhara and Angot.

According to local history, a Jewish Queen by the name of Yodit (Judith) or "Gudit" overcame the kingdom and burned the churches and literature around c. 940. Scholars have found proof that there was indeed an invasion around that time period; however, many doubt that Queen Judith ever existed since they can't find any evidence that she did. However, another explanation for the invasion and eventual burning of churches was that a pagan queen by the name of Bani al-Hamwiyah of either the al-Damutah tribe or the Damoti tribe (Sidama) was responsible. Regardless of who it actually was and where she came from, modern history claims that a feminine usurper took control of the state during that time, and she ruled up until the year 1003 when her reign came to an end. Then, the empire plunged into a dark age, albeit short-lived, after which it was succeeded by the Agaw Zagwe dynasty, considerably smaller in size and landmass, in the 11th century or the 12th century (probably in 1137). The last king of Zagwe was killed by a man named Yekuno Amlak, and it was he who founded the contemporary Solomonic dynasty sometime in 1270. Yekuno Amlak discovered that he had a right to rule after he traced his ancestry to the last king of Aksum known as Dil Na'od. One thing is worth mentioning here, the fact that the Aksum Empire ended does not mean that its culture, traditions, and works of art ended as well; for instance, there is a huge influence by the empire on Zagwe dynasty architecture at Lalibela and Yemrehana Krestos Church.

Climatic Change Hypothesis

There are also some claims that the change in climatic conditions, as well as isolation in trade and economy, was what led to the decline of the Kingdom of Aksum. There was a climatic shift in the 1st century CE, which led to an increase in the local resources; more rainfall came about during spring such that it rained for six or seven months rather than the usual three and a half months. This greatly brought about an improvement in the supply of water both on the surface and subsurface, resulted in a doubling of the growing season, and created an atmosphere that could be compared to modern-day Central Ethiopia where two crops can be cultivated in a single year without the need for irrigation. This is probably the reason why the external environments of agriculture in Ethiopia were able to support the population, thus creating a very powerful commercial kingdom. It could also be the reason why no rural settlements expanded into the more fertile and productive lands of Begemder or Lasta when the kingdom was in its season of great agricultural prosperity. When profits from the international trading network dwindled, it became difficult for the kingdom to control its sources of raw materials, and that led to the eventual collapse of the trade networks.

The pressure that was already placed on the environment to provide for the kingdom's large population was further increased, and this only brought about soil erosion that started on a local scale in c. 650 and grew in magnitude by c. 700. The problem became intensified due to socioeconomic inputs, which was shown in the decline of maintenance on the land, deterioration and part desertion of land that could be cultivated, destructive exploitation of pastures, and eventually, wholesale and land degradation. All of these were brought about by a decline in rainfall between c. 730, and c. 760, the result was the reestablishment of a short growing season during the 9th century.

Foreign Relations, Trade, and Economy

The Aksum Empire was greatly involved in the trade network that existed between India and the Mediterranean (Rome, later Byzantium) since it had a territory that spanned over today's northern Ethiopia and southern and eastern Eritrea. Some of the goods being exported from Aksum included ivory, tortoise shells, gold, and emeralds, while imported goods include silk and spices. As a result of the empire's access to the Red Sea and the Upper Nile, its navy was able to acquire huge profits from trade between different states in Africa (Nubia), Arabia (Yemen), and India.

The major goods that Aksum exported were agricultural products as these were the mainstay of that period. Compared to what it is now, the land was more fertile in ancient times, and the major crops being grown were grains like wheat and barley. Livestock farming in Aksum included raising animals like cattle, sheep, and camels; Aksum people were also hunters – they hunted wild animals to obtain ivory and rhinoceros' horns. Countries with which Aksum had transactions include Rome, Egypt, and Persia. Other resources that the Kingdom of Aksum had in abundance were gold and iron – both of them were very valuable materials to trade – but there was one other item that was just as valuable, it was salt. Since the supply of salt was quite large in Aksum, it fetched the empire significant trade with other states.

The transformation of the Indian Ocean trading system in the 1st century was of huge benefit to the empire as it provided a direct link between Rome and India; in the former trade system, there was a need for voyages along the coast and various go-between ports for goods to be exported or imported. At around 100 BCE, a route was established to link Egypt and India; this called for the use of the Red Sea and using winds of the monsoon season to cross the Arabian Sea into the southern part of India. The volume of trade, and thus sea traffic, that occurred across this route grew to a huge extent, more so than was the case on older routes as of 100 CE. The sudden rise in the demand for goods from southern India by Romans led to a large number of big ships traveling down the Red Sea from Roman Egypt to the Arabian Sea and India.

The idea behind the location of the Kingdom of Aksum was so that the kingdom could be in a position where the new trade circumstances would be more favorable towards it. Not long after, Adulis turned into a port where all kinds of goods were exported, such as ivory, gold, incense, slaves, and various exotic animals. In a bid to ensure the constant supply of these goods, the kingdom's emperors made sure to develop and expand a good inland network of trade. However, as with all trading networks, there is usually a rival, and this time, it was the Kingdom of Kush, which like the Aksum Empire, worked the interior region of Africa and was the major supplier of goods to Egypt via the River Nile. Be that as it may, the 1st century CE saw the complete takeover of the territory that previously belonged to the Kingdom of Kush by the Aksum Empire to the extent that ivory that was collected from Kush was exported through the port Adulis rather than being taken to Meroë, which was the Kush capital city. In the 2nd and 3rd century CE, Aksum went on to expand its control over the southern Red Sea basin. A wagon route to Egypt which bypassed the Nile was created. The Aksum Empire then achieved the feat of being the major supplier of African products to the empire of Rome partly because of the transformation of the Indian Ocean trading system.

Society

The people of Aksum were made up of people who spoke the Semitic language known as the Habeshas, people who spoke the Cushitic language, and people who spoke the Nilo-Saharan language such as the Kunama and Nara. Cultivation of land was performed in a reformed feudal system.

Culture

There are a couple of areas that the Aksum empire was quite famous for, and some of them include its alphabet and the Ge'ez script, which was later reformed to have vowels in it and eventually became an Abiguda. In addition, about seventeen hundred years ago, the people of the empire constructed obelisks, which were called "stelae," and these were used to mark the tombs or grave chambers of kings and noblemen of the kingdom. One of such obelisks is the most famous, known as the Obelisk of Aksum.

During the reign of King Ezana, the kingdom adopted the Christian religion in c. 325 to replace the polytheistic and Jewish religion that it was previously practicing; and this was what brought about the Ethiopian Orthodox Tewahedo Church – which gained independence from the Coptic Church in 1959 – and the Eritrean Orthodox Tewahedo Church – which received independence from the Ethiopian Orthodox church in 1993. Since the separation from the orthodox form of the church after the Council of Chalcedon in c. 451, the church became a very significant Miaphysite church; also, the scriptures and liturgy of the church still remain in Ge'ez.

Religion

The Aksum empire used to practice a polytheistic religion, which had relations with the religious practices of the southern part of Arabia before the kingdom then converted to Christianity. While they practiced the polytheistic religion, one of the items they used for worship was the crescent-and-disc symbol that was used in southern Arabia as well as the northern horn. Other sources of history claim that the pagan people of Aksum used to worship Astar, his son Mahrem and Beber.

There also exists an argument that a major change in religion came upon the Aksumites such that the only remaining old god was Astar; the other gods were substituted for a "triad of indigenous divinities" such as "Mahrem, Beber and Medr." More so, it is believed that the culture of the Aksum empire was greatly shaped by Judaism in that "the first carriers of Judaism reached Ethiopia between the reign of Queen of Sheba BCE and conversion to Christianity of King Ezana in the fourth century AC." It is further believed that "a relatively small number of texts and individuals dwelling in the cultural, economic, and political center could have had a considerable impact" and that "their influence was diffused throughout Ethiopian culture in its formative period" despite the fact that Jewish culture was greatly present and in a large magnitude. During the time when Christianity had completely found its footing in the 4th century, most of the Hebraic-Jewish elements had already been massively accepted by the indigenes of the state and were no longer seen as foreign. In addition, they were not even thought of as posing a threat to the acceptance of the Christian religion.

Before he converted to the Christian religion, the coins, as well as inscriptions of King Ezana II, depict that he may have offered worship to the gods Astar, Medr/Meder, Beher, and Mahrem. However, there is yet another inscription that shows that Ezana was totally Christian because it made reference to "the Father, the Son, and the Holy Spirit." It was King Ezana II's teacher by the name of Frumentius who converted him to Christianity in the year 324 CE; it was also Frumentius who established the Ethiopian Orthodox Church. Frumentius was the emperor's teacher when the emperor was yet a boy, and it is believed that this set the stage for the conversion of the entire kingdom to Christianity. The evidence that points to the conversion of the empire was the replacement of the crescent and disc to the cross on their coins; be that as it may, the Jewish people of Aksum did not accept the new religion, and they created the Kingdom of Semien in rebellion. Frumentius, while having contact with the Church of Alexandria, was later appointed to be the Bishop of Ethiopia at around 330 CE.

The Church of Alexandria did not have much influence on the churches that were in Aksum, and this allowed the Aksumites to develop their own special form of Christianity. This doesn't entirely mean that there was no influence at all in the sense that, when the Church of Alexandria did not accept the Fourth Ecumenical Council of Chalcedon, churches in Aksum also backed them up, thus creating the Oriental Orthodoxy. There are certain claims that the holy relic known as the Ark of the Covenant was rested in Aksum; these claims suggest that the Ark was laid for safekeeping by Menelik I, in the Church of Our Lady Mary of Zion.

Islam entered the empire in the 7th century under the rulership of Ashama ibn-Abiar when followers of the Prophet Muhammed endured persecution from the tribe that was in power, and since the king offered them shelter, many of them migrated. In the year 622 CE, all of them went back to Medina.

Ethiopian Sources

Sources from Ethiopia, like the Nebra Nagast and the Fetha Nagast, claim that Aksum was a kingdom with Jewish culture. In the Nebra Nagast, there is a story of how the Queen of Sheba or Queen Makeda of Ethiopia met the King Solomon of Israel and a trace of Menelik I of Ethiopia, who was the son of both Queen Sheba and King Solomon. The Nebra Nagast is in itself a very old source of history (more than 700 years old), and many historians, especially those of the Ethiopian Orthodox Tewahedo Church, consider it to be a reliable source.

Coinage

Among the various states in Africa, the Kingdom of Aksum was one of the first to mint its own coins, which eventually created a legend in Ge'ez and Greece. From the time when Endubis reigned down to the reign of Armah (approx. c. 270 to c. 610), minted gold, silver, and bronze coins were already in existence. A state's ability to mint its coins was considered a huge feat in ancient periods; it meant that the Kingdom of Aksum saw itself as equal to its neighbors. Most of the coins were used to depict the events taking place whenever they were coined. For instance, the addition of a cross to the coin was used to show that the kingdom had then been converted to the Christian religion. Furthermore, with the availability of coins, it was easy for the kingdom to engage in trade, and at a certain point, proved useful when it was necessary to gather information and obtain profit.

Architecture

Generally, all the major buildings in the Kingdom of Aksum, like the palaces, for instance, were built on top of podiums that were constructed out of loose stones made to stick together with mud mortar. The corner blocks were made of granite that had been cut in little pieces, which rabbet to almost an inch at steady lengths the higher the wall was; as a result, the walls were narrower, the higher they went. The podiums upon which these buildings were constructed were usually what was left among the ruins of the Aksum Empire. The walls built upon the podiums were mostly made of loose stone placed in an alternating fashion, and these stones were usually coated with whitewash as is the case in the Yemrahana Krestos Church; there were horizontal beams that had smaller rounded beams in the stonework usually sticking out of the stone walls – referred to as "monkey heads" – on the outer side of the house and sometimes the inner side as well.

In the end, the podiums, as well as the walls, were no longer straight as they rose up; instead, there were indentations at steady lengths such that, for any wall that was high, there were areas where the stonework showed concavity and areas where they just protruded from the walls. This was done so that the walls would be much stronger. The architectural features of the houses in the kingdom such as columns, doors, windows, bases, capitals, pavings, staircases on the flank of the walls of the pavilions in the palaces, water sprouts – which mostly had the shape of a lion's head – were created out of worked granites. Doors and windows were usually made of stone or cross-members of wood, each of which was connected at the corner either by square "monkey heads" or small lintels. Some of these features were noticed in the carvings of famous stelae and rock-hewn churches of Tigray and Lalibela.

There was always a central pavilion in the palace, which usually had other substructures that were all around it; the structures also consisted of pierced doors or gates, which made sure that the occupants (kings and nobles) had some level of seclusion. The biggest structure among them all is the Ta'akha Maryam, with a measure of 390 feet in length by 260 feet in width. However, since it was discovered that the pavilion it had was smaller than those in other palaces, it was summed up that the structures of other palaces were bigger.

Certain houses made of clay serve as a representation of what small settlements used to be like in the old days. For instance, a round hut with a roof shaped in the form of a cone with layered thatches can be observed while another is a rectangular hut with the doors and windows also rectangular in shape; there are beams ending in "monkey heads" to support the roof, and then, there is the breastwork with a water spout on the roof of the house. A square-shaped house and somewhat pitch-looking thatches to serve as the roof can also be observed.

Stelae

The major part of the architectural legacy of the Kingdom of Aksum that is most easily identified are the stelae. The stelae were stone slabs used to mark graves, and they were also used to symbolize a huge and majestic palace with multiple stories. The decorations on the stelae are false doors and windows that are designed in Aksum's style of artwork. The largest one of the stelae measured 108 feet in height, if not for the fact that it broke eventually. Most of the mass of the stelae is usually kept above ground; be that as it may, they are supported by counterweights below the surface. On the stone slabs are usually engravings that have a certain pattern or design that indicates the rank of the king or the noblemen.

Chapter 6

Sahelian kingdoms

The Sahelian kingdoms were a group of centralized empires or kingdoms located on and around the Sahel – a region of land with grasslands situated in the south of the Sahara – between the 8th and 19th century. These kingdoms acquired their wealth through trade as they were in control of the trade routes that ran through the desert. The power of the kingdoms was drawn from the possession of sumpters such as camels and horses, which were fast enough to ensure that the entirety of these large empires remained under a central authority; they were also used for battles when the need arose. Although these empires were a lot less centralized, in that cities that were members of the empires enjoyed independence from the center.

The Sahelian kingdoms faced restrictions when it came to the expansion of their territories toward the south and into the forest zone of the Bono and Yoruba because warriors mounted on animals were useless in forests, and the horses, as well as camels, were not able to withstand the diseases that plagued those regions.

Economy

The Sahelian kingdoms had integrated empires that had many cities and important towns, although their territories were not very organized and their populations were rather dispersed. The people practiced agriculture, rearing of livestock, hunting, fishing, and various crafts such as metalwork, textile, and ceramics. They traveled across rivers and lakes doing trade in both short and long distances, and they had their own currencies for exchange.

History of Sahel kingdoms

Among all the Sahelian kingdoms, the Ghana Empire was the first major empire to rise in prominence. It was established in the 8th century, and it was located in what is now modern-day Senegal and Mauritania. The Ghana Empire was also the first kingdom to derive benefit from the pack animals that were introduced by Wolof traders. The period between c. 750 to c. 1078 was the period of the predominance of the Ghana Empire in the region. The smaller kingdoms during this period were Takrur, which was located west of the Ghana Empire; Malinke kingdom of Mali, which was located toward the south; and Songhai and Gao, which were located east of the empire.

After the kingdom of Ghana fell into demise, certain smaller kingdoms took over, one of which is the Sosso. By the year 1235, the Mali Empire became the most powerful nation in the region, engaging in trade with the Bono state, which was located toward the south. The Mali Empire was located on the River Niger, west of the Ghana Empire at a location now occupied by Niger and Mali; the kingdom of Mali reached the zenith of its predominance in the 1350s, however by 1400, the empire had lost the control it had over some of its feudatory states.

Among the Sahelian kingdoms, the most powerful was the Songhai Empire, which expanded its territories quickly starting during the reign of King Sonni Ali in the 1460s. By the year 1500, the empire had land stretching from Cameroon to the Maghreb and was the largest kingdom in the history of Africa. However, the empire did not stand for long as in 1951, the empire crumbled due to the fact that it was attacked by a Moroccan army unit (musketeers).

Deep into the east, on the Lake Chad, rose another very powerful empire known as Kanem-Bornu, although when it was founded in the 9th century, it was only known as Kanem. To the west of Kanem were the barely united Hausa city-states that also became predominant. Both of these kingdoms had an anxious coexistence between them; however, they both were stable.

With the coming of the year 1810, the rising of the Fulani Empire came about after it had conquered the Hausa, it then created an empire that was more centralized. Both the Fulani Empire and the Kanem-Bornu continued to coexist.

Sahelian Kingdoms

Kingdom of Alodia

Alodia was a kingdom located in the region of modern-day central and southern Sudan. The capital of the kingdom was Soba, which is located in what is now Khartoum at the point of convergence between the Blue and White Nile Rivers. The kingdom met its demise in 350 CE.

Bamana Empire

The Bamana Empire was a Sahelian kingdom that was located at Ségou, which is now a part of Mali. It was founded after the great Mali Empire and the Keita dynasty waned. The empire had a strong economy because trading with other nations boomed. The Kulubali or Coulibaly dynasty ruled the kingdom.

Kingdom of Baol

The Baol Kingdom was one of the kingdoms to rise out of the division that the Wolof Empire faced in the year 1555. The capital of the city was Diourbel, and that was the dwelling place of the kingdom's ruler, Teigne. The territory that the kingdom possessed spanned from the ocean to the capital city, and some of the towns include Touba and Mbacke. The Kingdom of Baol was located toward the south of the Cavor Kingdom, and from the Kingdom of Sine, it was located toward the north.

Kanem-Bornu Empire

The area of land which was occupied by Kanem-Bornu is what is now present-day Chad and Nigeria. It was once famed the Kanem Empire to Arabic geographers during the 8th century CE, and it became the Independent Kingdom of Bornu or (Bornu Empire) until 1900. The Kanem Empire (which was what it was known as between c. 700 to c. 1380) spanned over modern-day Chad, Nigeria, and Libya. At the pinnacle of its existence, the Kanem Empire covered the majority of Chad, a portion of southern Libya (Fezzan), Eastern Niger, northeastern Nigeria, and the northern part of Cameroon. The Bornu Empire, which lasted between the

1380s to 1893, at some point became larger in terms of territory than Kanem in that it spanned over a portion of Chad, Niger, Sudan, and Cameroon; although as of today, the empire is now in the northeastern part of Nigeria.

Daju

Oral traditions have it that the Daju are a people who arrived in Darfur from either the east or the south, probably the region of Shendi in Nubia. The language of the Daju people sounds a lot like that of the Nobim. They established a kingdom in southern Jebel Marra, and from that location, they exerted their influence and power over the neighboring states in regions that were located toward the south and south-east. According to the Arab historian al-Idrisi, the Daju people were camel breeders.

Funj Sultanate

The Funj Sultanate was a kingdom whose territory spanned across present-day Sudan, the northwestern part of Eritrea, and the western part of Ethiopia. The kingdom was established in the year 1504 by the Funj people; Islam was the religion of the kingdom. The pinnacle of the kingdom's existence was the 17th century; however, that height was short-lived because, in the 18th century, the kingdom declined and finally crumbled.

Ghana Empire

The Ghana Empire existed from c. 300 up to c. 1100, and the proper name for the empire was Wagadou – this was also the name of its ruler. It was a kingdom that was located in West Africa in a place that is now currently southeastern

Mauritania and western Mali. There were a lot of states in the region that engaged in the trans-Saharan trade selling gold and salt in ancient times; however, when camels were introduced into the western Sahara in the 3rd century, it brought about major changes in the region, which then resulted in the Ghana Empire. During the period where Islam conquered all of North Africa in the 7th century, the use of camels had paved way for the emergence of unusual trade routes and as well as a trade network that ran from Morocco to the Niger River. This trans-Saharan trade of both salt and gold made the Ghana Empire very rich; afterward, bigger and better urban centers started developing. The increase in trade volumes also brought about expansion in territory, in a bid to secure control over other trade routes.

The actual emergence of the dynastic rulership of the Ghana Empire is not known; written history only mentions it in the year 830 by Muhammad ibn Mūsā al-Khwārizmī. A scholar by the name of al-Bakri from Cordoba traveled to the area in the 11th century and then recorded in detail a description of the empire.

During the empire's decline in the 13th century, it became a liege subject of the Mali Empire, which was rising at the time. When the Gold Coast became the first nation in sub-Saharan Africa to gain its independence from colonial powers, it renamed itself Ghana as a way to honor the empire that had been lost.

Origin

The earliest discourses regarding the origin of the Ghana Empire can be found in the Sudanese chronicles of Mahmud Kati and Abd al-Rahman al-Saadi. Kati's work depicts that twenty kings ruled Ghana before the coming of the Prophet, and the empire even lasted over a century after the Prophet. According to him, the rulers of the empire came from one of the three following origins: Soninke, Wangara (this is a Soninke group), and Sanhaja Berbers.

The 16th-century interpretations of the genealogies of kings of the empire linked Ghana to the Sanhaja original interpretations; al-Idrisi, an 11th-century writer, and ibn Said, a 13th-century writer, both believed that the rulers of the Ghana Empire drew their ancestry from a clan of the Prophet Muhammed either through Ali, his son-in-law or Abi Talib, his protector. According to ibn Said, twenty-two kings reigned over the empire before the Hijra, and afterward, twenty-two others reigned. Although these early views give a certain unusual interpretation of the origin of Wagadou, they are most often not well regarded by scholars. For instance, al-Idrisi's view is not well regarded because his work shows that there were glaring miscalculations in geography and historical chronology; on the other hand, al-Kati's and al-Saadi's view is argued to have stemmed from nomads who trespassed the territory after the demise of the empire, mistaken to be members of the original population. Furthermore, it is argued that al-Kati and al-Saadi totally ignored or did not give enough amount of consideration to the accounts of modern-day writers who all report that the population and rulers of the Ghana Empire to be "negroes."

History of Islam in the Ghana Empire

Contemporary scholars have since time past had a long and lasting controversy about how vast the empire of Ghana was and how long the kingdom stood. Islam was a religion that was very prominent in the Asian-African-European region. According to Abu-Abdullah Adelabu, who is an African

Arabist, non-Islamic authorities on history do not regard the significance of how the territory of the Ghana Empire expanded because they do not want to acknowledge the fact that Islam had a serious influence on the empire. In one of his books, the scholar states that Muslim historians and geographers in Europe such as Abu-Ubavd al-Bakri from Cordoba have had their works suppressed in order for opposing views of non-Islamic Europeans to be held. He noted the refusal of the non-Muslim Europeans to recognize Ibn Yasin's *Geography of School Of Imam Malik* that contained a detailed account of activities in the Ghana Empire, both social and religious, which have established concrete evidence of a bias in the composition of documentations of the empire's history by European historians especially because they relate to Islam and Muslim societies in ancient times. In the words of Adelabu:

> The early Muslim documentaries including Ibn Yasin's revelations on ancient African major centers of Muslim culture crossing the Maghreb and the Sahel to Timbuktu and downward to Bonoman had not just presented researchers in the field of African History with solutions to how scarce written sources were in large parts of sub-Saharan Africa, it even consolidated confidence in techniques of oral history, historical linguistics and archaeology for authentic Islamic traditions in Africa.

Oral Traditions

During the latter part of the 19th century, colonial officers started to collect accounts of the tradition of the ancient Ghana Empire, and some of those accounts include manuscripts that were written in Arabic; it was during this time that French troops occupied the region. Most of these traditions were not only recorded but also published. The traditions stated that the empire was established by a man whose name was Dinga, who emerged "from the east" and continually migrated to a number of various places in western Sudan; and for each place he settled, he left children after having a wife there. In a bid to acquire power at the final place he settled, he had to slay a goblin and then become married to his daughters, who eventually became the ancestors of clans that had more influence and control in the region at the time. After the death of Dinga, Khine and Dyabe, who were both his sons had a contest for the empire's rulership; Dyabe won the contest, and thus, the kingdom was founded.

Koumbi Saleh

Koumbi Saleh, which is on the border of the Sahara Desert, is believed to be the place where the capital of the Ghana Empire stood. According to the way in which al-Bakri describes it, the capital was actually two towns that were separated by "continuous habitations" of about six miles such that they were sometimes thought of as being merged to become one.

El-Ghaba

The major part of the city in the ancient Ghana Empire was El-Ghaba and that was where the king resided. With a stone wall to protect it, it played the function of being both the royal and spiritual capital of the kingdom. There lay in the city, a sacred grove where priests resided as well as the palace of the king, which also happened to be the largest building in the city and it was surrounded by other "domed buildings." Also, in the city, lay a single mosque for when Muslim officials came visiting.

Muslim District

No record of the name of the second part of the city exists; however, wells having fresh water in them surrounded it because that was where vegetables were cultivated. Most of its inhabitants were Muslims; there were twelve mosques, one of these mosques was built primarily for Friday prayers, and it had a complete group of scribes, scholars, and legal experts. Most of the Muslims in this part of the city were merchandisers; this is why some think that it was the principal business district. It is very probable that the merchants were black Muslims referred to as the Wangara or, as they are called in the modern day, Dyula and Jakhanke. The practice of running towns or cities that are autonomous of the influence of the main government is something that can only be attributed to the Dyula and Jakhanke Muslims in all of history.

Economy

The majority of the knowledge that pertains to the economy of the ancient Ghana Empire was obtained from al-Bakri. According to him, all the businessmen were mandated to pay a tax of one gold dinar on all sports importations, and for export, they had to pay two gold dinars. As for other commodities, the dues were fixed, and this included copper. Most of the imported goods were likely textile materials, ornaments, and other products. The designs of many of the leather goods that were handcrafted and found in Morocco were traced to the empire. Koumbi Saleh, the empire's capital, was the major center for trade. The ownership of all the solid gold in the empire was claimed by the king, leaving only gold dust to the people. The influence of the king was exercised upon local regions; as a result, the different chiefdoms and tributary states had to pay tributes to the outer boundary of the empire.

When camels were introduced into the trading system, it paved the way for the success of the Soninke in that goods could be transported in a more efficient manner over the Sahara. All of these factors helped the empire to remain a powerful state for some time, bringing about an economy that was not only stable but also wealthy, thereby facilitating its survival for centuries. The empire was also very well known for being a hub for education.

Decline

Considering that the sources from which the story of ancient Ghana was gathered are scattered in nature, there is no way to determine the exact period of the decline of the empire. The quondam sources that describe the empire are unclear; however, as al-Bakri noted, the kingdom had forced Awdaghost in the desert under its rule between years 970 and 1054. At the time of al-Bakri, the empire was already bordered by powerful kingdoms like Sila, and by the year 1240, the kingdom had already become a part of the Mali Empire, thus establishing its end.

According to a tradition in historiography, the demise of the Ghana Empire was brought about by its pillaging under the hands of the Almoravid movement, which took place in 1076 and 1077 in spite of the resistance that the Ghanaians posed towards the attack for approximately ten years. However, this tradition was disregarded by Conrad and Fisher

(1982), who are of the opinion that the attack launched by the Almoravid troops was nothing but a myth that was derived from misinterpretation or unenlightened dependence on Arab sources. Although there are some scholars who disagree with the arguments of Conrad and Fisher, the fact remains that there is no archaeological proof that the Ghana Empire underwent any radical change, neither is the decline of the empire in any way linked to the era of conquests of the Almoravid army.

Notwithstanding the unclear evidence that the Ghana Empire was conquered, sources of the empire's history give an account of the nation's conversion to Islam as documented by al-Idrisi, who wrote down the information he gathered in the year 1154, and at the time, the entire state was already Muslim. A North African authority in history by the name of Ibn Khaldun, who referenced the work of both al-Bakri and al-Idrisi, stated that the power of the Ghana Empire started to dwindle as the power of the "veiled people" began to rise, via the Almoravid movement. The report that was given by al-Idrisi did not provide grounds that the empire was facing demise or that its power was weakening at the time he published the report, which was seventy-five years after al-Bakri had already published his own account; instead, al-Idrisi described the capital of the empire saying it was "the greatest of all towns of the Sudan with respect to area, the most populous, and with the most extensive trade." The only clear information was the account of al-Umari in the year 1340, which recorded that the Ghana Empire was adopted into the empire of Mali. After it was incorporated into the Mali Empire, Ghana remained a kind of kingdom with its ruler being the only person permitted to bear the name Malik and was "like a deputy" to the Mali emperor.

Aftermath and Sosso Occupation

Ibn Khaldun recorded that after the Ghana Empire converted to Islam, "the authority of the rulers of Ghana dwindled away and they were overcome by the Sosso [...] who subjugated and subdued them." Later traditions believe that from the late 19th century to the 20th century, Diara Kante assumed leadership of the Koumbi Saleh, and afterward, he founded the Diarisso Dynasty. Soumaoro Kante, son of Diara Kante assumed rulership after his father and forced the citizens to pay tributes to him. The Sosso also took over the territory of its neighbor to the south, the Mandinka state of Kangaba, in which the major goldfields of Bure were sited.

Malinke Rule

In the brief record given by ibn Khaldun regarding the history of Sudan, he noted, "The people of Mali outnumbered the peoples of the Sudan in the neighborhood and dominated the whole region." He continued saying that Mali "vanquished the Sosso and acquired all their possessions, both their ancient kingdom and that of Ghana." Modern tradition has it that Sundiata Keita was the leader of the Mali revivification (Sundiata Keita was the man who established the Mali Empire and was the swayer of its core region, Kangaba). The tradition further notes that Ghana, who was then a feudatory of the Sosso, decided to hoist a rebellion against Kangaba, after which it became a member of a group of Mande-speaking lands. After Soumaoro was defeated at the Battle of Kirina (1235, an arbitrary year assigned by Delafosse), the new swayers of Koumbi Saleh became complete allies with the

Empire of Mali. With the accompaniment of Mali's growth in power, the role of Koumbi Saleh as an ally was reduced to that of a mere subservient land.

Empire of Great Fulo

The Empire of Great Fulo, or as it was also called, the Denanke Kingdom, was a Pulaar kingdom of Senegal that existed before the coming of Islam. The kingdom was in control of the Futa Tooro area, and it exercised dominance and influence over the neighboring kingdoms via the use of its military as well as through the wars it fought with the empires of Mali and Songhai.

Jolof Empire

The Jolof Empire or the Wolof Empire was a kingdom that was based in what is now the nation of Senegal. For almost two centuries, the rulers of this kingdom received tributes from its liege states, who agreed to become liege states without being forced. The kingdom's demise stemmed from the defeat of the Buurba Jolof by the lord of Kavor at the Battle of Danki.

Kaabu Empire

The Kaabu Empire was a large empire that was located in the region of Senegambia and had territory spanning what is today the northeastern part of Guinea-Bissau, the majority of present-day Gambia, and down to Koussanar, Koumpentoum, parts of southeastern Senegal, and Casamance in Senegal. The kingdom was once an imperial army state of the Mali Empire.

Kingdom of Kano

The Kingdom of Kano was a Hausa kingdom that existed before 1000 CE in the north of present-day northern Nigeria. It stood for a long time until it was proclaimed the Sultanate of Kano.

Mali Empire

The Mali Empire was established by Sundiata Keita; it existed between 1235 to 1670. The Mali Empire started as a small state of Mandinka in the upper regions of River Niger. It was between the 11th and 12th centuries that it evolved into an empire after the decline and fall of the Ghana Empire. In 1670, Bamana invaded and burned down Niani, and not long after, the Mali Empire fell.

Mossi Kingdoms

The Mossi kingdoms were a group of powerful nations in present-day Burkina Faso that had control over the Upper Volta River for many centuries. These kingdoms were established as a result of the marriage of warriors from the Mamprusi area of today's Ghana with the women in the region.

Kingdom of Saloum

The Kingdom of Saloum was a Serer/Jolof kingdom based in what is today's Senegal. The rulers of the kingdom probably originated from Mandinka/Kaabu. The capital city of the state was Kahone, and it was a sister kingdom to Sine. The history, culture, and geography of both kingdoms were connected such that they were referred to as Sine-Saloum.

Shilluk Kingdom

The location of the Shilluk Kingdom was along the White Nile River bank in today's South Sudan. The capital of the city, which was the ruler's residence, was Fashoda. Folk history has it that the kingdom was founded by its first ruler, who was a demigod by the name of Nyikang.

Kingdom of Sine

The Kingdom of Sine was a Serer kingdom that was located on the bank to the north of the Saloum River delta in present-day Senegal. Inhabitants of the kingdom were known as *Siin-Siin* or *Sine-Sine*.

Sokoto Caliphate

Sokoto Caliphate was an autonomous Sunni Muslim caliphate that was established during the jihad war of 1804 by Usman Dan Fodio in West Africa. At the pinnacle of its existence, this kingdom connected more than thirty emirates and more than ten million people into one kingdom. It was among the most important empires in 19th century Africa.

Songhai Empire

The Songhai Empire was a kingdom that exercised dominance of the western Sahel during the 15th and 16th centuries. During the time the kingdom was at its pinnacle, it was among the largest empires in the history of Africa. The empire was forced to go down when plots and coups were used to ascend the throne during the reign of the Askia dynasty.

Sultanate of Darfur

The Sultanate of Darfur was a kingdom before the colonial era in what is now Sudan. It existed between the year 1603 and October 24, 1874 at which time it fell into the hands of Rabih az-Zubayr who was a warlord from Sudan. At the height of its existence, which was the late 18th to early 19th century, the kingdom spanned over Darfur down to Kordofan and the western banks of the White Nile; thus, it attained territory as large as modern-day Nigeria.

Pashalik of Timbuktu

The Pashalik of Timbuktu was established in 1591 when military troops of about three or four thousand soldiers plus auxiliaries from Morocco left Marrakesh, overcame the Songhai army at Tondibi, and subdued Gao, Timbuktu, and Dienné. Timbuktu was made the capital. In 1787, the Tuareg subdued Timbuktu, and Pashalik was made into a tributary.

Tunjur Kingdom

There are no records of how the Tunjur kingdom was established; however, it is known that the kingdom substituted a previous Daju kingdom. The lands under the control of the Tunjur kingdom spanned across modern Sudan and even up to present-day Chad. In the early 16th century, it ruled over Darfur and Wadai.

Wadai Sultanate

The Wadai Sultanate was a sultanate in Africa that was located toward the east of Lake Chad in modern-day Chad and the Central African Republic. It was during the reign of the first sultan, Abd al-Karim, that the kingdom emerged in the 17th century after subverting the Tunjur people in the area.

Wassoulou Empire

The Wassoulou Empire, also referred to as the Mandinka Empire, was an empire in West Africa whose establishment was built upon the conquests of Malinke ruler, Samori Ture. The empire did not stand for long, existing only between 1878 and 1898.

Chapter 7

Mali empire

The Mali Empire flourished as a trading empire in western Africa from the 13th to 16th century; it is known as one of the largest empires in the history of West Africa. At its peak, the Mali Empire stretched from the Atlantic coast to parts of the Sahara Desert (central areas). From historical studies, the Mali Empire was birthed in 1235 CE and thrived until the 1600s CE. The rise of the empire was preceded by the short-lived Sosso Kingdom ruled by Sumanguru Kante. The Sosso King successfully conquered several Malinke kingdoms that were part of the ancient Ghana empire (which is not related to present-day Ghana) located around the upper Niger River in the early 13th century. Before their conquest, the Malinke, including those in Kanganba, were middlemen in trades, especially the gold trade.

The Sosso king or chief (as he is sometimes referred to) became infamous due to his harsh, oppressive, and ineffective rules. This provoked the revolt by the Malinke resistance under the leadership of Sundiata in 1230 CE. Sundiata is believed to be the brother of Kanganba's fugitive ruler. In 1235 Sundiata and his army defeated the king of Sosso, Sumanguru Kante. Many historians, including the likes of

Innes Gordon and Conrad David, believe 1235 was the birth year of the great Mali Empire, whose history is still being discussed in oral traditions. The birthplace of Sundiata Niani became the capital of the empire, and from there, he extended through the Atlantic Coast located south of the Senegal River all through to Gao, located east of the Niger bend.

King Sundiata deployed imperial armies to subdue the lands to the south of Bambuk and Bondu. These territories were known as "gold-bearing land." To the northeast, Diara was overcome, and the imperial armies continued north along the Niger to Lac Debo, still under the rule of King Sundiata. While under Mansa Musa, the Mali Empire rose to its greatest height. Mali conquered the famous trading cities of Gao and Timbuktu. Mansa Musa also took over the towns Taghaza and Walata that were very rich in salt deposits to the north and south Sahara, respectively. The Mali Empire extended its rule over its eastern borders to include the Hausa people. The peoples of Tukulor and Fulani, including Takrur, were conquered to the western borders. In places like Egypt and Morocco, ambassadors and imperial agents were sent to represent the emperor.

Administration

Sundiata laid the foundation for the administration that every other emperor would build upon. All through the history of the Mali Empire, the king, also referred to as mansa, was assisted by an assembly of local chiefs or elders. This assembly, headed by the mansa, held meetings either indoors in the palace or outdoors under a tree in the presence of the audience. The mansa had supreme or absolute powers over the judicial system, and he acted as the only source of justice. The mansa never had legal advisors but he had ministers that helped in in the day to day running of the empire. Some of these ministers include the master of the treasury (this was formerly called granaries), the chief of the army, the royal orchestra leader, and the master of ceremonies. Although the king had these ministers, he was supreme and had monopoly power over important trades. Some of the trades the king had a monopoly over include; gold nuggets. All other traders had to deal in gold dust.

The king was believed to have magical powers, which caused his citizens to be loyal to him and his slaves exclusively loyal. Whenever the king ate, no one was permitted to be in his presence, and all visitors had to come before the king barefoot, bow down and sprinkle dust on their heads before coming to him. The king's leadership was like that of a cult and could not be questioned or debated. This resulted in a highly centralized system of government. The fate and fortune of the empire depended solely on the king. If the king was talented (like Mansa Musa), the empire would progress, and if it lacked talent, the empire would suffer. Under Sundiata, the empire progressed and incorporated Walata, the old kingdoms of Ghana, Songhai, and Tadmekka. Niani, which was located around the Sankarani River, was chosen to be the capital of the empire.

Apart from the fact that Niani was the birthplace of Sundiata, Niani was chosen because of its strategic location. Niani was surrounded by mountains, which gave it a military advantage. Another strategic advantage of Niani was that it was very close to major areas like waterways and forests, which acted as sources to trade goods (such as salt and gold).

After conquering a place, local chiefs who were loyal were left to continue ruling their people while the disloyal ones were replaced by someone else from the chiefdom who was loyal. To ensure that local chiefs remained loyal, they were assisted by a governor appointed by the emperor. The governors had control over a garrison stationed in the conquered territories.

The Mali Empire ensured continued loyalty by taking members of the royal class as hostages and remanding them in Niani, the capital. Every chiefdom was expected to pay tributes to the emperor, and the appointed governors oversaw this. The Mali Empire had a very functional administrative system, which was the reason it flourished and attained the height of the wealthiest empire in Africa's history. The Mali Empire's wealth astonished both Arabia and Europe. Visitors from Europe and Arabia were also astounded by the high level of justice they noticed in its society. They also experienced an uncommon level of security and safety, as visitors could move around freely and conduct trade without fear of being attacked. In all villages of the empire, food was in abundance.

Military

The Mali Empire developed a highly trained and powerful military. This is heavily reflected in the frequency and number of its military conquest beginning from the late 13th century and all through the 14th century. The initial organization of the military is credited to Sundiata. Although subsequent emperors inherited a very functional military, the empire's military underwent a series of important changes before it could attain its legendary status that was the envy of all. These steady and radical changes were made possible by two things: the first was the steady influx of taxes, which was used to service the military and equip them with the most sophisticated weapons; the second was the stability and continuity in government that began in the concluding part of the 13th century all through to the 14th century. These reasons were also behind the advancement of the empire's power within and beyond its boundaries. The empire's army was highly organized and had a special elite corps of horsemen. It also had numerous foot soldiers in every battalion. The military was charged with the responsibility of protecting the empire's flourishing trade by defending its borders from external and internal attacks.

The weapons used by the army were largely dependent on the region of origin of the troop. And because the empire was vast, it would be accurate to say that the empire's army made use of several kinds of weapons. Among all its troops, the sofa were the only ones directly equipped by the capital, and they heavily made use of bows and arrows (poisoned). The Mandekalu troops from the north were equipped with shields made of animal hide and short spears for stabbing, known as tamba. Warriors from the south were also armed with bows and poisoned arrows. The bow was a prominent symbol in the Mali Empire's warfare as it was used to symbolize military force. The garrison and field armies were largely made up of bowmen. In fact, in Kaabu, the troops had a ratio of three bowmen to one spearman. The bowmen made use of arrows that were iron-tipped and mostly poisoned. In addition, bowmen were equipped with a knife and two quivers that were tied behind their arms. For siege warfare, the empire's army made use of flaming arrows. The infantry was equipped with bows and spears and the cavalry was equipped with foreign and locally made lances and swords. The imperial army also had as one of its weapons, poisoned javelins that were heavily used in skirmishes. Horsemen wore helmets made of iron, mail armor for their defense, and carried shields that were similar to those carried by the infantry.

The empire mandated every clan to provide a quota of fighting-age men whenever the emperor demanded. These men were freemen known as the Horon caste, and they were expected to come with their own weapons. That way, the empire maintained a quasi-professional full-time army always on standby to defend or advance its borders. Historians record the empire's army's peak to be one hundred thousand, with cavalry making up ten thousand. The armies could be deployed on short notice throughout the empire with the help of the water clan. There are numerous historical sources that affirm that war canoes and other vessels for war transport were used frequently in the inland waterways of West Africa. Most of these canoes were constructed using single logs or carved out from a big tree trunk.

The imperial armies were later divided into two divisions, known as the southern and northern commands. These commands were under the command of the sankar-zouma and farim-soura, respectively. These leaders were both members of the emperor soldier elites that were referred to as "ton-ta-jon-ta-ni-woro." The ton-ta-jon-ta-ni-woro was a squad of sixteen slaves who carried quivers. These warrior elites had a representative known as ton-tigi (quiver master). At the Gbara, each of the ton-tigi was charged with providing counsel to the mansa or emperor, but among the ton-tigi, sankar-zouma and farim-soura had more powers, and it is even believed that all other ton-tigi were under them.

These ton-tigi were members of a special force that was made up of cavalry commanders known as "brave men" (translated from farari). These commanders had a team of individual farariya or "braves" under their command. Each farariya was made up of some infantry captains or officers referred to as duukunasi or kele-koun. In battle, the duukunasi or lele-koun were responsible for leading troops under the command of a "brave man" (farimba) or a "great brave man" (farima), respectively. Apart from their commandant, another slight difference is that unlike the kele-koun who led freemen, the duukunasi led sofa, a slave troop responsible for guarding the horses. The farimba carried out their duties from the garrison under the protection of the entire slave troops. While on the other hand, the farima carried out its operations on the battlefield with all freemen.

Economy

Just like the Sosso Kingdom and the ancient Ghana Empire before it, the Mali Empire flourished for two major reasons; strategic location and trade. The empire was located between the rain forest in the southern part of West Africa and the Islamic caliphate in the northern part of Africa. The empire's interior was readily accessible through the route provided by the Niger River to the Atlantic Coast. While from the north, the empire traded goods, and this was made possible by the Berber-controlled camel caravans, which crossed the Sahara Desert. As mentioned earlier, the Mali Empire had three main sources of revenue, which were acting as middlemen by buying goods and selling at a much higher price, taxes for passage of goods, and access to valuable natural resources. Among these natural resources were gold found in the regions of Bambuk, Galam, and Bure under the sovereign rule of the empire. With the control of the resources, the empire had a rich foreign exchange. Gold dust was exchanged for salt in the Sahara. As the development of minting coinage in precious metals progressed in places such as Italy (precisely Genoa and Venice) and Spain (Castile), gold was in high demand.

Another trading opportunity was opened to the Mali Empire in the wake of the 14th century. This opportunity came as a result of the conquest and incorporation of territories in the inland Delta, such as the eastern Songhai and Gao. These provinces contributed greatly to resources from farming, hunting, fishing, and grazing. Also, these new provinces were sources of slaves for the military, slaves for trade, and slaves for production. Also, the empire's treasury felt the impact of the addition of these two new provinces as tributes from their chiefs and kings were paid to the empire to pledge their loyalty. The conquest of these provinces also meant the control of new trade routes, which translated into the payment of tariffs to the empire. When Mansa Musa ascended the throne in the mid-14th century, he embarked on numerous pilgrims to Cairo. On his trips, he was extravagant in his spending and gifting, and this publicized not only his wealth but the wealth of the empire throughout North Africa, the Middle East, as well as Europe. The stories that were told about the empire's wealth attracted many traders to the Sahara. In fact, there are historic documentations that Egyptian traders were frequent visitors to the Mali Empire. One such evidence was the Malians in Walata, which was a commercial center, wearing imported clothes from Egypt. This outcome is believed to have been the result of Mansa Musa's pilgrimage. The Mali Empire also extended its trade to the Maghreb region. This was achieved under Mansa Musa, who exchanged embassies with the sultan of Morocco. Among the commodities that were traded in the trans-Saharan trade route were salt, slaves, ivory, animal hides, copper, and gold (which was the most prestigious commodity). European, North African, and Middle Eastern monarchs competed for gold in the trans-Saharan trade, which the Mali Empire had control over and dominated.

The conquest and incorporation of the trade center Timbuktu also boosted the economy of the empire. Timbuktu was founded by the Tuaregs (nomads) in the 12th century. Under the nomadic Tuaregs, Timbuktu acted as a quasi-independent trade port. The port had two advantages: one was that it was located in the Niger River bend, and two, it was where the trans-Saharan caravan started from. When the Mali Empire took over Timbuktu, they upgraded to be one of the most cosmopolitan and important trade centers in the history of Africa. Important and luxurious goods such as weapons, textile, kola nuts, ivory, glassware, sugar, sorghum, spices, millet, craft products, military, transportation horses, and slaves were traded in Timbuktu. In some instances, goods were exchanged with other goods (trade by barter). While other times, goods were paid for using the generally or personally acceptable currency, which could either be gold ingots or copper, an agreed quantity of ivory or salt, or cowry shells obtained from Persia.

Rulers

Ibn Khaldun and Abu Abdullah Muhammed ibn Battuta are among the three historians (and geographers) who equipped the followers of history with detailed documentation of the Mali Empire during the medieval era. Some of these scholars documented the power and greatness of the Mali Empire to be second to none throughout the history of Western Sudan. Sundiata or Sunjata became king after successfully revolting and defeating the Sosso or Sosso kingdom. He is believed to be the greatest Mali king ever. According to records, he ruled for about twenty-five years.

Mansa Wali, his son, succeeded him, and he as well, according to historical beliefs, was a great king. Mansa Wali was renowned mostly for his pilgrims to Mecca from around 1260 to 1277, which was during the period Sultan Baybars reigned. Like most African kingdoms or empires, the Mali Empire went through a series of leadership tussles. And unlike most, she endured and was able to reach her peak. Mansa Wati, who was a brother to Mansa Wali, succeeded him, although Mansa Wati had nothing special documented about him. Mansa Wati was succeeded by Mansa Khalifa, who was another brother to Mansa Wali. Mansa Khalifa had special attributes that he is remembered for. But all were negative. Mansa Khalifa was believed to be an insane king who had no respect for the life of his citizens. In fact, he would use them as targets for archery practices. Mansa Khalifa was assassinated by his own people, who grew tired of his insanity. He was succeeded by Mansa Abu Bakr. Mansa Abu Bakr's mother was a sister to the three mansas that preceded him, which means she was a daughter to Sundiata. It is a common belief among historians that the problem of the empire began from about this time, as would be proven by the next mansa.

Mansa Abu Bakr was succeeded by Mansa Sakura, who was not a member of the royal family. He was a military commander who is believed to have had the support of the majority due to the ineffectiveness of the royal family. He also made pilgrims to Mecca, a journey that took months from Mali. Historians draw their conclusion of Mansa Sakura having the support of the people from his journey to Mecca; they believed that there was no way he could have afforded to be away from the empire for that long if he wasn't popular among the people. Sakura is known to be one of the greatest kings of the empire as he stabilized the empire politically. This had a positive effect on trade, thus increasing the empire's prosperity. Mansa Sakura is also credited with the expansion of the eastern borders to include the territory of Songhai. Many believe Gao was conquered during his reign as well. Mansa Sakura was killed in one of his pilgrimage to Mecca. After his death, the kingship reverted to the royal family and precisely to descendants of Sundiata. Two successive descendants of Sundiata ruled with no records worthy of note. They were succeeded by a descendant of Mansa Sundiata's brother, whose name was Manden Bori. He was a Muslim and had Abu Bakr as his Arabic name.

Mansa Musa I

Mansa Musa was a descendant of Maden Bori, and he is believed to have brought the empire back to its golden age after years of failed leadership. Mansa Musa established an imperial army of about one hundred thousand men, among which ten thousand of those men were armored cavalry corps with horses. He had Saran Mandian, who was very skillful in the act of warfare as his general. With this force, Mansa Musa could not only enforce his rule within his territory, but he would also go ahead to extending the empire's frontier. Historians believe that under the rule of Mansa Musa, the territories of the Mali Empire were doubled. He extended and enforced the empire's rule on all sides of its borders; to the east, he re-enforced the empire's control of Gao that was located along the Niger River. To the west, he extended his rule to the lower parts of Senegal and Gambia. The forest situated in what came to be referred to as the Gold Coast and the region of Bure were conquered and controlled by the empire to the south. To the north, which is along the western

Sahara, every tribe was subdued, and as the empire grew, so too did the religious, linguistic, and ethnic features.

Under the administration of Mansa Musa, detailed records were kept, and copies were sent to the central office located in Niani, which was the capital. Mansa Musa ruled the empire and its diverse people by personally appointing governors known as farba. These governors were in charge of allocated provinces. They were to collect taxes, peacefully settle disputes, including tribal, and provide justice in their provinces. Under Mansa Musa, the empire prospered greatly because tributes were coming to the capital from trades, tributes from conquered chiefs, sales of natural resources. The empire had so much wealth that the king single-handedly crashed the price of bullion by 20 percent by giving away so much gold on his visit to Cairo in 1324 CE. This resulted in the rumor that spread as far as Spain in c. 1375 that the streets of Mali were littered with gold. In fact, in the first-ever European detailed map of West Africa, the land of Mali was branded as a huge reserve of gold, with Mansa Musa wearing an enormous crown made of gold. These rumors have a lot to play in kindling the interests the Europeans later developed in West Africa and Timbuktu, the great trading city.

Mansa Sulayman

Mansa Musa was succeeded by his son Mansa Magha in 1337. But Mansa Magha was only king for four years before his death. He was succeeded by Mansa Sulayman, who was his uncle. Unlike Mansa Musa, who was loved by his subjects, Mansa Sulayman was very unpopular as the people didn't like him. Although he was unpopular, he was very skillful in the act of leadership and was powerful. During the reign of Mansa Sulayman, Ibn Battuta, the Arab geographer, visited Mali between 1352 to 1353. So, there is much information available about the empire administration under the rule of Mansa Sulayman. Sulayman reigned from 1341 to 1360 and during his reign, audiences were held that permitted the citizens to come and present their complaints or disputes before the king. Some of these audiences were held in the royal court. This court was described as a "lofty pavilion" that had gilded arches on the side and long curtains by Ibn Battuta. The curtains were raised, and a flag hung outside the window, drums were beaten and trumpets blown before the king would sit. Other times, the audience was held at the base of a giant tree.

The king's throne was elevated with stairs, and a shade made of silk with a golden falcon placed on top of it was constructed over the throne. The falcon on top of the shade is similar to the one in the king's court. When the audience was held either in the king's court or under the tree, royal dignitaries and members of the king's cabinet would sit in the presence of the king. Outside, the honor guards numbering three hundred would line up according to their ranks, half of them armed with bows and arrows, and the other half with lances. Outside the palace, two rams were always present, which were believed to protect the king by warding off witchcraft. Also, there were always present two saddled horses that the king could decide to use at any time. Whenever the king appeared in public, he always wore a golden headdress and carried a bow and quiver, which was a symbol of power in Malian culture. Immediately after the king ascended the throne, his councilors, deputies, and all subordinate kings were summoned to come before the king before having their seats. All the king's subordinate kings had their own entourage made up of his personal honor guard armed with bows, quivers, and lances, and as they and their entourages walked towards the king, there were trumpeters and drummers marching in front of them.

Mansa Mari Jata II

Mansa Sulayman was succeeded after twenty-four years as king by his son Mansa Kanba in 1360. That same year, there was civil unrest because of the power tussle between Kanba and his cousin, Mansa Musa's son. This resulted in a civil war in the same year Mansa Kanba ascended the throne. Mansa Kanba died in 1373; he only ruled for nine months. He was succeeded by Mansa Mari Jata, who was the son of Mansa Magha and the grandson of the great Mansa Musa. Some historians believe Mari Jata was the same person invited by Kasa to overthrow her husband, Mansa Sulayman.

The succession struggle seed was sown during the reign of Mansa Musa. When Mansa Musa would go on a pilgrim, he would leave Magha in charge and when he died, Magha succeeded him; Mansa Musa's brother was grieved because he expected to be the next mansa being the most senior male in the family. Mansa Magha ruled only four years and he was then succeeded by Mansa Sulayman. Some schools of thought believe he was murdered by Sulayman. This, they say, could explain the reason the people disliked him and also the reason his wife would invite Jata to overthrow her husband.

Mansa Mari is known to be the most despotic king the Mali Empire ever had. He inflicted his people with much pain and suffering. He ruined the empire by destroying the principles of justice his predecessors had ruled by. Jata also depleted the empire's treasury. Among all his atrocities, the most infamous was the selling to Egyptian traders the empire's huge gold nugget at a meagre price. This gold nugget was the Mali Empire's most valuable national treasure. Mansa Jata died in 1373 after suffering from sleeping sickness.

Religion

The Mande society, which included the Mali Empire, had always believed in the spiritual realm. And this spiritual belief affected every area of their society, from their personal relations to carrying out trade. Traditionally, these people believed their relationship with inhabitants of the spirit world was affected by either their actions or inactions. In fact, several supernatural creatures had a specific name; now, they could all be referred to as jinn in Arabic, which was translated to genies. But as trade increased and caused the mixture of several cultures and religions, one of the religions that entered into West Africa through trade was Islam. Islam was introduced by Arab merchants who came to trade. There are two contrary records of when Islam became the official religion in the Mali Empire (that is, which of the kings first converted to Islam). One report is given by the Muslim chroniclers and travelers, Ibn Khaldin and Ibn Battuta, while the other comes from the oral tradition of the Malinke people.

While the former recorded that Sundiata, who was the first mansa, converted to Islam. The latter refutes the claim that Mansa Sundiata converted to Islam and abandoned their indigenous religion. It was, however, recognized that Islam was already in Mali even before the reign of the first monarch. It is recorded though that Mansa Uli, also known as Mansa Wali, Sundiata's son, went to Mecca as a pilgrim in the 1270s. This was followed by subsequent Mali kings as a tradition. The Malinke oral tradition is kept by the griots (special bards) from generation to generation.

Mansa Musa's reign is believed to be the peak of the Mali Empire's Islamization. He frequently pilgrimed to Mecca, and on his return, he brought back Islamic books, scholars, and even architects. These scholars taught in the Koranic schools as well as higher institutions he built. Although, the curriculum went further than just religious studies to include courses such as astronomy, history, medicine, and geography. These educational institutions rose to gain international recognition. The architects he brought designed buildings like the ones he saw in Mecca, which included mosques. For example, the "great mosque," also known as Jingereber, was located in the cosmopolitan city of Timbuktu. The architects also designed great libraries containing thousands of manuscripts and books. Islam further spread into West Africa due to the influx of Muslim clerics into the region; these clerics were attracted to the region by the number of new converts. Also, citizens from Mali who converted to Islam traveled to Fez in Morocco to study, and many turned out to be great scholars, saints, and missionaries to neighboring territories. When indigenes of the region embraced Islam, the religion moved from being a foreign religion to one of Africa's religions.

Although Islam had gained ground in the entire region, the rural areas continued to practice their indigenous religion. This was recorded by Ibn Battuta in one of his visits to the Mali Empire in c. 1352. One of the reasons the indigenous religion continued to strive was that Islam was unpopular because it was only taught in Arabic and not in their local language. For this reason, Islam flourished only in the educated class and cities. Another reason Islam could not flourish in the rural areas was that it wasn't able to completely replace the Malian's ancient animist belief. This had an effect on the Islam that was practiced in Mali as many believed it to be adulterated and slightly differed from the one practiced in the Arab world.

Culture

The griots (storytellers) were custodians of the Malinke's legends. They were also responsible for orally transferring the empire's histories from generation to generation, even to this present day, and they mixed the stories with music. According to the Malian Empire's culture, there were special songs composed and sung only for some reputable citizens. This was the case for very talented and accompanied hunters and warriors. Sculptures made of solid pottery and usually measuring up to twenty inches in height were produced in areas like Djenne. These sculptures were sometimes made solid by adding iron rods to the interior. Other materials used for the production of sculpture include brass, wood, and stone. Paints were used to make decorations. Among the figures sculpted were warriors with beards riding on a horse. Other sculptures were crouching figures with faces turned upward; some of these sculptures were used for burial and ritual ceremonies, while others were used for decorating homes of wealthy citizens.

Decline

The Mali Empire flourished from the 13th century, and at the end of the 15th century, it began to decline. Just like every other empire before it, its progress and advancement attracted rivalry from neighboring kingdoms, and one of such kingdoms was the Songhai. The empire was also attacked in 1433 CE by the Tuaregs. Aside from the several attacks, the major reason for its disintegration was that it had no strict and defined laws for succession among members of the royal family. This led to succession conflicts between brothers and uncles and sometimes resulted in outright civil wars. Other attacks on the empire include the attack by the inhabitants of lands located to the south of Niger River, the Mossi people.

The Mali Empire was reduced to a shadow of its former great self. Due to the strong competition between European kingdoms for the control of West Africa, which would result in the control of the Saharan caravans, the one who controlled the caravans would control the most effective means of transporting goods (including slaves) to the Mediterranean. This competition and the presence of the Europeans reduced the authority the Mali Empire once had in the region. In 1468 CE, the Songhai Empire, at its peak under the reign of King Sunni Ali, attacked and conquered the Mali Empire.

Chapter 8

What is left today of classical african kingdoms

Among the many kingdoms that existed in precolonial Africa, only a few of them are still standing today. In the whole of North Africa, for instance, none of the ancient kingdoms are still existing; in the Horn of Africa, only the Sultanate of Aussa and the Tooro Kingdom still stand. In West Africa, only the Asante Union still exists, while the Kuba Kingdom is the only empire that is still standing in Central Africa.

East Africa

Kingdom of Buganda

This empire is one from which the Ganda (Uganda) people emerge. It happens to be the largest empire in all of East Africa. The kingdom was called the name Muwaawa, before the coming of the 12th century.

Sultanate of Aussa

The Sultanate of Aussa was adopted into Ethiopia in 1945; however, the empire still had rulers appointed over them under the Ethiopian government. Therefore, the kingdom still had a certain level of independence between the 1950s and 1970s. Still today, the domain is under the Sultan's rule, the current Sultan being Hanfere Alimirah, who succeeded his father in 2011.

Tooro Kingdom

After it was established in 1830, the Kingdom of Tooro was incorporated into Bunyoro-Kitara in 1876. The people of the kingdom known as Batooro speak the same languages as the Bunyoro people; their cultures also have similar features.

West Africa

Asante Kingdom

The Ashanti Kingdom was established in 1695, and it is still standing today. It is a subnational empire that is protected by the constitution since being joined with the Republic of Ghana. Presently, it is being sustained through its dealing in cocoa, kola nuts, agriculture, and gold bars.

Central Africa

Kuba Kingdom

The Kuba Kingdom is a kingdom that is populated by people of the following tribes: Kete, Coofa, Mbeengi, and the Kasai Twa Pygmies. It is home to a total of nineteen separate tribes even to date. The ruler of the kingdom is referred to with the title *Nyim*

Chapter 9

Conclusion

There is no doubt that kingdoms that existed in Africa before the coming of colonists were great empires having large and prosperous civilizations during their peak. They were mostly involved in the trade of items such as salt, ivory, textile materials and so on; some of them were able to mine gold from their lands.

Since the precolonial African empires were self-sufficient, they traded with European merchants for textiles and other commodities; and the Europeans who visited these kingdoms often marveled at how their governments were centralized and how well the rulers conducted their authority. A good number of these kingdoms conquered their neighbors in order to expand their territory and they became great enough to threaten European powers.

However, most of the precolonial kingdoms were affiliated in that they met their end (the kingdoms fell) due to a number of reasons, which include internal disputes among tribes, struggle for power among the rulers as well as priests, and the arrival of colonial masters.

Did you enjoy the book? If so, please **leave a positive review** directly on Amazon!

Do you want to get rid of stress and learn something new in the process? Discover the new series **"Myths and History Coloring Books"** and you'll find the perfect way to do that. So what are you waiting for?

Scan the following QR code and take a look!

Printed in Poland
by Amazon Fulfillment
Poland Sp. z o.o., Wrocław
25 October 2022

90ac51c7-3cdb-433d-928c-bac1b63f3773R02